CREATIVE WRITING FOR COUNSELORS AND THEIR CLIENTS

STEVE FLICK, M.F.A., L.C.S.W.

1415 HERVEY STREET
BOISE, IDAHO 83705
208-869-7638
EMAIL: SAXMANFLICK@HOTMAIL.COM

CREATIVE WRITING FOR COUNSELORS AND THEIR CLIENTS
Copyright © 2009 by Steve Flick

1415 Hervey Street
Boise, Idaho 83705
saxmanflick@hotmail.com

All rights reserved. No part of this book may be used, reproduced or transmitted in any form or by any means whatsoever without the permission of the author or publisher except in the case of brief quotations embodied in critical articles or reviews.

ISBN: 978-0984190201

First Edition Printing

Design by:
McCabe Christian
Dogstar Creative, LLC.
www.dogstarcreative.com
info@dogstarcreative.com

Printed by:
Boise Metro Digital Printing
Boise, Idaho

Borderline Publishing
406 S. 3rd St
Boise, ID 83702
www.borderlinepublishing.com

Book Body Printed on SFI Certified Fiber Sourced Paper
www.sfiprogram.com

Table of Contents

How Creative Writing for Counselors Came About 1
The Therapeutic Nature of Creative Writing 4
Creative Writing and Inner Child Work 6
Inner Dialog and Depression 8
Interactive Creative Writing Exercises and Schizophrenia 11
Writing About Relapse Symptoms 12
Managing Voices 13
Bipolar Disorder 15
Basic Journal Entries for Self Discovery 16
Expand your Journal Writing with Prompts 20
Journal on a Personal Ad 22
Benefits and Drawbacks of Journaling 24
Poetry as Therapeutic Release 24
Poetry from a Depressed Teenage Girl 27
Checklist for a Mood Episode 29
Writing a "Sketch" 29
The Letter 29
Letter to Mom and Dad in Newspaper Form 30
Portrait of your Father / Letter to your Father 30
Letter to Your Father 32
Portrait of Your Mother 33
Letter to your Mother 35
Family Dynamics 35
Writing to Help People with Anxiety Disorders 36
A Marriage Gone Wrong: Anxiety from PTSD Deb's Journal 36
Rewrite Your Life 39
Writing for People with PTSD 43
Practicing with Feelings 45
Writing Dramatic Scenes and Dialogs for Therapy 48
To Be or Not to Be 48
The Exercises: Life Review 51
Living Will 53
Durable Power of Attorney for Health Care 55
Writing a Mission Statement 58
A Coming of Age Story: "Depth of Field" by Steve Flick 62
Analyze the Story Regarding Psychological Issues 66
Writing About The 12 Steps of AA/NA 67
"Scene from an NA Meeting" by Steve Flick 68
Group Story 71
Writing for Clients who Have Depression 73
How Old Are You, Really? 75
Analyze the Story About Childhood Sexual Abuse 77
The Play Room 78

Myograohy 80
The Victim Statement: A Step in Recovering From Trauma 88
Young People Writing About Their First Sexual Experiences 91
Writing About Relationships, Personality, Feelings, Family Drama 93
After the Happily Ever After 94
Personal Characteristics Inventory from an Online Matchmaking Website 95
Do a Genograph of your Family 97
Creative Mental Health Assessments 98
Personality Types 98
Scripts of My Life 100
Finding a Therapist if Your Writing Leads You to Know That You or Your Clients Need More Help 103
Happiness 104
Join a Writing Group, Take a Class, and Attend a Writer's Retreat 107
Paradoxical Intention or Injunction 107
The Creative Process 109
Enhancing Your Personal Creativity 110
Creative Writing About Money 112
What's in *Your* Wallet (or Purse)? 112
Letter to the Problem 113
The Classroom is the Garden of Daydreams: The Classroom is the Garden of Anxiety 115
Describe Your School Experience 117
Writing Assignments for Clients with Assorted Issues 119
The "Left-Brain" Approach to Understanding a Poem 119
Writing to "Vent" 121
L.H.'s Vent 121
The Author's Vent 123
A Left-brained Way to Analyze a Short Story 124
Creative Activities for Children to Write About 125
Family Feeling Log 126
Learning Log 126
Helping the Helpers: Writing About Burnout 126
What It's Like to Be Me 130
Point of View 131
Poetry Reading, Poetry Slam 131
Teaching Rap and Hip-hop 131
The Garrity Method for Group Therapy 133
Reading Out Loud 134
Thinking Errors Journal 134
Coming to Your Own Assistance 136
Afterword 137
Example for A Newsletter by Clients 139
Example for Therapeutic Writing Group 145
Influential Works 149

Loretta Pompeii Flick,
    Silversmith, Wife, Partner

This couldn't have been done without you.

How Creative Writing for Counselors Came About

Through my knowledge of writing and counseling I came to realize that a book had to be written which incorporates these two parallel activities. Writing and counseling supplement each other, to provide continuity for the counselor and client from one session to another. This book if full of writing projects which will help you, the counselor, apply them to your clients. This book was born of that knowledge.

There has always been a link between writing and psychology in my life. I began writing poetry in the seventh grade, imitating work I had read of William Blake. I wrote to gain the attention of my mom and dad and my teachers. My parents were also avid readers of psychologists who were contemporary during the 50s, such as Freud, Jung, Adler, Horney, Rollo May, Erikson, and so on. Somewhere in my child's brain I knew that writers and shrinks were people whom they admired, and that if I modeled myself after these people, I might also gain my parents' love and admiration. Later in my life I came to understand that they read psychology to heal the effects of deprived and toxic childhoods, set in the context of the Great Depression.

In college I read the A.A. Brill translation of The *Interpretation of Dreams* and *The Psychopathology of Everyday Life* by Freud, and came to admire Freud's writing ability, as well as his interpretive and analytical skills. This had a strong influence on me, particularly in the way Freud revealed how childhood traumas influenced behavior later in life. His theories were based on the plays of Sophocles from which he drew the Oedipus and Electra complexes, an important example of how creative writing and psychology have been mingled from the beginning.

In the context of the Vietnam War, I resolved my conflict of wanting to serve my country without killing people, and so declared myself a Conscientious Objector and was hired to work as a Psychiatric Technician at Agnew's State Hospital in San Jose, California in 1966.

As a Psych Tech I worked in a female geriatrics unit of Agnews for three months, learning to care for the physical and psychological needs of the aging, and I began to keep a journal. Part two of the training involved working with developmentally delayed clients, and part three consisted of a stint in the psychiatric facility for the chronically mentally ill. After Ronald Reagan was elected Governor of California, he began to dismantle the mental health care system there, and I went to work at the Veteran's Administration Hospital in Palo Alto, California, working with addicted vets who were returning to the U.S.

It was there I started keeping notes in my journal about the people I met, the experiences I had, and the goals and dreams I wanted to develop in my life. I began an autobiographical novel titled *The C.O.*, in which I developed and unified the experiences I had, working with the female geriatric patients at Agnews. I sent a second draft of *The C.O.* to Stanford University in June of 1968 and was awarded a Wallace Stegner Creative Writing Fellowship to Stanford during the 1969-70 school years.

Thus, the connection between creative writing and psychology became reinforced with the receipt of $6,500 for both the Stegner and the Book of the Month Club College English Fellowship during the summer of 1968. When I took the fiction writing course at Stanford and met Stegner and Richard Scowcroft, I was privy to the elite world of published writers, agents, and publishers who visited the Palo Alto campus. Ken Kesey had just left the campus and was on the way to publishing *One Flew Over the Cuckoo's Nest*, a book set in a mental hospital in Oregon. I believed I was on track for publication and for living the life I'd dreamed as a writer.

The next year after I had finished *The C.O.* my own agent, Bob Dattila in New York, admitted that he had trouble dealing with the subject matter of the geriatrics ward and also admitted that "I felt bad about not being able to deal with it." I realized I had to do something to make a living and began applying to graduate school programs in creative writing. The two I chose were the University of Iowa and the University of Montana. In 1972 I was accepted to the latter and in August of 1973, I packed my belongings, invited my girlfriend to go on this adventure and took off for Missoula in a VW, pulling a small trailer behind us.

When I attended the U. of M., I found out that one of my teachers, Ed McClanahan, had been instrumental in selecting my novel *The C.O.* for the Stegner Award at Stanford. I studied with Ed, Dick Hugo, Madeleine Defrees, Bill Kittredge, and students from all over the

1

country. I met Robert Tate, Ken Kesey, and many other writers who stopped in Missoula to read their works and sell books.

Before leaving for Montana, I had begun Primal Therapy at the Primal Institute in San Rafael, California where my sister had previously received treatment and later became a Primal Therapist herself. I had begun to realize that my writing carried much anger and guilt from my divorce and from leaving my twin sons. In my journals I noticed the effect of the unresolved issues with my mother and father. I had a therapist at the U. of M. named David Devine who helped me understand the connection between my family of origin, my guilt and anger, and the breakup that first summer with my girlfriend.

As I look back over those times now, it's clear to me that the guilt interfered with all of the creative impulses I was learning to harness into fiction. It also set up a self-defeating dynamic in my relationships. Instead of being able to get decent feedback, I think I was carrying a kind of "chip on my shoulder" which made it difficult for others to give me feedback.

I believe that some writers who get blocked are grappling unconsciously with guilt issues which are trying to get to the surface, and therapy can help writers and clients confront the guilt. There is some anecdotal myth floating around that therapy eliminates or reduces a writer's ability to create, but as I have found in my own life, if one has a good therapist, it only enhances creativity. Janov used to say therapy helped writers to feel their feelings, rather than to simply symbolize them in fiction and poetry, and if therapy changed anything, it might be the content of what was written, not the style.

As I learned in the 90s, I also possessed an undiagnosed case of Adult Attention Deficit Disorder which kept me turning to other activities, such as music, teaching, and counseling, when the going got tough with my writing. Then, I came from a family dynamic where the communication was split down gender lines: my dad and I were close, and my sister and mother were close. I learned to write what I thought and felt, but not to say it out loud. I learned to escape into my journal, my music, and my fiction. As a young boy I recall being alone a lot and having to learn to entertain myself with my imagination and music.

As I continued to write, I knew there was something "wrong" with me, I just didn't know what. Writing helps the writer or client eventually figure out "what is wrong" with him or herself. And for years, this inability to communicate in person to those around me left me with one defense, which was to leave. Also, ADD presents problems in relationships which are related to the constant need for stimulation and new partners.

After graduating from the U. of M., I moved to Eureka, California and worked in a lumber mill. Eventually, I got job teaching English as a Second Language at Humboldt State University and began my teaching career. Teachers were a "dime a dozen" then, and so I moved to Hawaii with my second wife and began teaching writing and literature at the University where I finally got a full time job at Windward Community College. I was able to support myself and there began to write again, short stories and poetry, and I began my second novel *Teller's Last Band*.

During this period, literary criticism included Freudian analyses of not only the characters in fiction, but also the writers who produced it. One of my early role models was John Cheever who wrote short stories for the *New Yorker*, including "The Swimmer" which later became a movie starring Burt Lancaster. Later on, Cheever discovered his homosexuality by falling in love with a prisoner who attended one of his creative writing classes at "Sing-Sing" in Ossining, New York. Cheever's daughter discovered his secret life in his journal after he died, and learned about Cheever's notorious womanizing and cheating on his wife nearly all of their marriage. This is an example of Freudian criticism in the 60s through the 70s, which included discussions of unconscious conflicts revealed in the stories belonging to the authors. Cheever once remarked that writing was an important avenue through which one could gain understanding of oneself.

When I met Loretta, my third wife, in Hawaii I was already in counseling with an extraordinary woman named Kate, and she helped me finish the grieving, acting out, and non-committal behaviors which had prevented me from succeeding for nearly forty years of my life. I started a novel that summer and my mother helped by paying my child support. I bought a synthesizer with my retirement money, and began teaching myself to play keyboard. I cried, wrote, and talked my way through my middle-aged crisis with Kate and Loretta's help, and got married under a Mango Tree. Kate was primarily the role model for my deciding to become a therapist. We used my journal extensively in therapy sessions to enhance the processing of feelings and to express my feelings in person to people around me in an appropriate way.

I worked with Loretta in her pool service while in San

Diego, taught English part time at a community college in Chula Vista, and played some music with a local rock band. Burnout became a problem for me because there were so many part-time instructors willing to work without benefits we became known as "*freeway flyers,*" darting up and down Highway 5 putting together a schedule at two or three campuses, just to make a living. In 1993 I took a GRE test and passed; then, I applied for graduate school, and filled out an application for a Federal IV-E Fellowship working with At-Risk children. Luckily I was accepted at Boise State University, and by the time we reached Boise, I found out that I had been awarded the Fellowship.

Before I left for graduate school in 1994, I began revising my novel Teller's Last Band, and I put together a men's workbook called *The Feeling Process: A Workbook for Men*, hoping to publish some work involving the men's movement. By then I was sure that my fiction-writing dream had come to an end, and that I was finally going to get some training in a field where I could work one-on-one helping people as a counselor.

Thus, my education has come full circle during the past fifteen years of working with clients. I have caught up with the changes in counseling and therapy techniques, done research, worked with over a thousand children, teens, adults and couples in hospitals, clinics, schools, and private practice. I am amazed and humbled by these experiences, and I have watched clients grow and change by using the materials in my book.

This introduction needed to be written because in counseling and in therapy, it's necessary to share some of one's life in order to model "self disclosure" to the people in the field who will be reading this book. What follows is the product of the experiences I have had in nearly 15 years of counseling and therapy, during which creative writing in the broadest sense has aided the process.

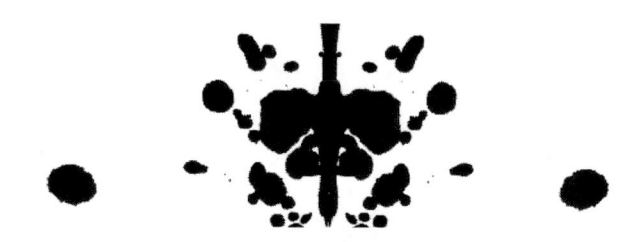

The Therapeutic Nature of Creative Writing

Creative writing is part of the Jungian archetypal human desire to tell stories. Even though we live in a technical world, we can still be transfixed by a story from someone who has practiced the craft of writing or who simply has lived a good story. Tapping into that storytelling energy can allow clients with identity issues, with economic and social marginalization, and the tragedy of early neglect, and physical and sexual abuse, to learn to work through their issues and tell the stories they have to tell. We all have an urge to tell our story or stories to the world. Sometimes this is completely oral, as in therapy, and some times it is done in writing, and sometimes in art.

The link between creative writing and therapy is two-fold. The first link is the perception involved in noticing and understanding character. From the *Bible* to *The World According to Garp*, the understanding of how a character exists in time as thoughts, feelings, and behavior is crucial both to therapists and to writers. As you read this visualize David and Goliath, Garp and Roberta, the transvestite former football player, Pip and Scrooge from Dickens. The storyteller captures a human being in words.

The second link is dialog, both outer dialog and inner dialog. Therapists and writers need to understand these dialogs because they reveal the extent of damage in self-esteem that their characters or clients are experiencing. The writer captures the symbolic meaning of these dialogs by showing characters in situations in which the dialog has a context. The therapist helps the client understand how the client can track and use the inner dialog to connect him to his or her true feelings. Berne's book *What do you say, After you Say Hello* focuses on his wonderfully apt description of this process from "skull rapping" to "scripts", which are entire life blueprints which run through generations of families.

For me there has always been a connection between writing, self-discovery and Psychology. When I began teaching English as a Second Language and college composition at Humboldt State University, I realized that I was borrowing my approach from Eric Berne's Transactional Analysis by using, the three stages of my classroom focus, based on Berne's concepts of Child, Adult, and Parent (CAP). Berne, after all, borrowed CAP from Freud's construct of Id, Ego and Superego, only he made it quantifiable through identifying ego states and inner dialog of patients. This theory also helped me on my journey towards understanding my own background and behavior.

Creative writing deals with a crucial issue in therapy, which is the difference between appearance and reality, dream states and awake states, the surface and the depths of the psyche. "A writer has to have a build-in shit detector," said Hemingway of writers in general, and the same is true of therapists guiding clients into dealing with reality. This is a very volatile area because a therapist has to ask the client to give up his or her fantasies and then has to help her appreciate and value reality. The popular culture is teaching its audience to follow its dreams, but it does not show the day-to-day steps one has to take to achieve a dream. The steps begin to teach the client the difference between fantasizing about becoming a musician and the reality of being one.

Creative writing can assist a therapist in helping clients to unblock the Critical Parent. Julia Cameron writes in *The Artist's Way* that "In order to tap into your creativity, you need to find it" (1992, p. 10). Finding one's creativity involves learning how to remove or silence the critical inner Parent. She recommends writing the "morning pages," three pages of longhand writing, strictly stream-of consciousness. "Although occasionally colorful, the morning pages are often negative, frequently fragmented, often self-pitying, repetitive, stilted or babyish, angry or bland, even silly sounding." She says the morning pages are the primary tool of creative recovery because they help externalize the critical Parent which stands in the way of blocked creativity and self expression: "Through the morning pages you learn to evade the Censor" (Cameron, 1992, p., 11).

The stream of consciousness writing is the "free association" method Freud introduced with his patients as one of the techniques for helping clients get in touch with their unconscious. Ken McCrorie's book *Telling Writing* introduced free writing into the teaching of composition as a primary way to reveal that writing is a process that has identifiable stages, and that the first stage is simply to get words on paper. It's also a way to help students and clients with writer's block. Free association is the process wherein the imagination allows images from the unconscious to the conscious awareness, similar to how dreams process material from the previous day. Writing helps in capturing the true thoughts, feelings and images and helps move aside the censor.

The morning pages of free writing teach logic brain (Critical Parent) to stand aside and let the artist or feeling brain play. "Anyone who faithfully writes morning pages will be led to a connection with a source of wisdom within," Cameron says. The issues in one's life emerge on the page and the writer or the client has to look at them. The way issues become clearer to writers and clients is simply because one day you discover you have written something to yourself, which you may have written over and over in whatever format you've chosen, and you realize you have to do something about it!

In therapy or counseling, the counselor does not have to respond to the writing as a literary critic. Response to creative writing is very different from that of a writing instructor or a critic. Don't get hung up in labels, formalities, rules, or strictures when prescribing writing assignments for clients. Even though I think Ira Progoff's journal approach is far too anal retentive for me, it still might work for about 15% of your clients who have highly developed left brains and need a structure to work within. Whatever format a client finds within which to express him or herself, that's the one to use. Whenever guidelines are suggested, it's always OK for the client to deviate from them as long as he puts something on paper. You might find one particular format which could unravel a whole set of repressed memories tucked away in the client's unconscious.

Creative Writing gives one a sense of control over one's world, because in many ways it is a reconstruction of one's reality which one can remake the best way possible, or the clearest way possible. Events in the client's lives can be reworked in writing to produce a different outcome. The abuse can be turned into courtroom drama, during which the abuser is tried, convicted, sentenced and begins a sentence wherein he is placed with a cellmate who perpetrates the same crime on him as he perpetrated on the victim.

Creative Writing and Inner Child Work

A creative writer spends a great deal of time with imaginary characters, interacting with them, rendering them with exquisite details which help bring them alive for us. This is similar to the way a schizophrenic child would create imaginary playmates to populate his or her world. He/she must get into the feelings, thoughts, backgrounds and behaviors of characters like and unlike him or herself. In my book *Teller's Last Band* I had to imagine what it would be like to be the gay waiter in the T.G.I. Friday's, waiting on the heterosexual couple as they are making out during lunch. I imagined what it would be like to kill someone, the way Teller has to kill Jason Darcy during the last chapter of the book. A writer in a sense creates a whole world in which he is God, and then when the work is finished, he or she must go on to fashion a new world and let go of the last one. The writers of fiction and poetry are like schizophrenic children with imaginary friends they have the power to share with the rest of us. That's how fiction becomes truth.

The "Inner Child" in Transactional Analysis refers first of all to the feelings, fears, and instincts we are born with. Another aspect involves the "natural" Child and the "adapted" Child. The adapted Inner Child acquires two shapes, the compliant and the rebellious child. Through the process of writing, each writer and each client learns to separate the tale from the teller (D.H. Lawrence) by separating childhood feelings from feelings which arise from the present. I will have more on that later in the book.

Every act of writing is an act of exposure, and getting used to that feeling is important in learning how to write without shame. Externalizing the negative "voices in our heads" is a process writer's experience daily. Clients also suffer from the childhood experience of being shamed as children when they tried to express their feelings. My clients come to me with that shame firmly ensconced in their inner and outer dialog. Creativity is so important to mental health because it always is related to the client's unique, individual self, and owning this self helps to reduce shame.

Creativity involves risk by taking a stand against the "internal censor" or Critical Parent. Clients and writers are often expressing dangerous ideas, such as doubting the existence of God (the ultimate Critical Parent), telling the truth about sexuality, dealing with suicidal ideation, exposing hypocrisy, and simply revealing the vision and points of view they have about life as it is. The duty of written art is to "imitate life." Art is not required to express the vision of the way things "ought to be" because that's the job of religion and philosophy.

It is the writer's and therapist's duty to establish a "non-judgmental zone" so that the reader or client herself can decide what the behaviors mean. If there is an agenda hidden within a poem, story, or novel, a judgment has been made about what the therapist or writer wants to direct the progress of the therapy. The judgment kills the story because it skews the details to fit itself. This is the most difficult part of creative writing because at a certain point in a revision, the characters acquire lives of their own, and they rise up off the page and begin to dictate to the writer what should happen next, according to the qualities the writer has imbued them with. Clients change in ways therapists did not envision when the therapy began. They have to learn not to judge in the beginning, so clients can unravel the narrative of their lives.

One condition of people in therapy seems to be that they have lost the ability to recall or be aware of specific details. This is also the process which has to be led by the Inner Child. The details of a traumatic experience, for example, can be the most traumatic part of that remembering. Those memories are released in therapy and writing and the pain along with them. For example, a rape victim will release the memory of the trauma while remembering some details, such as the smell, the feel or touch of her perpetrator in therapy, and that detail will trigger the whole experience.

Noticing the outside world helps clients climb out of their subjectivity. As I taught my writing students to notice from my Inner Child, so I began to notice. Clients and writers need to begin to see outside themselves. As each writer begins to notice, he or she begins to drag herself out of subjectivity into the outer world which others inhabit. That in itself is an excellent goal for therapy. When a client learns to reframe parts of her experience in Cognitive Therapy, she is putting a new spin or slant on her experience from an outside perspective.

Noticing details helps prevent helps the client from acting out of their subjective emotions. "What is the lesson, what did you learn from investing in real estate in Nevada without first checking to see if you had access to the land? Who does this man remind you of that sleeps with you but won't share his time, money or social life with you? Why are all your intimate experiences with abusive alcoholics? Why was this person in your life? To help you notice what you need, and to teach you to get it from someone who can give it to you.

Creative writing gives one some distance from the events and behaviors from childhood which are problematic. Sometimes this only comes as time passes. Sometimes writing just helps clients to "not take things personally." By writing the story of a traumatic incident, the rape victim can begin to gain control over the triggers, dreams, fears and other symptoms that come from PTSD.

Writing is a tool for lowering anxiety. There are parts of a personality which can improvise and mesh well with a group, but when the person is in "anxiety" mode, he or she will need a process to fall back on. It enables the person to rehearse the anxiety-provoking situation he will have to face. As a teacher I realized that if I wrote everything down, during anxiety mode, I had already prepared for the next assignment, the next "lesson," the next activity. Eventually I put it all in a composition workbook called *Speed Writing* which broke every phase of my class into steps.

There is a sense in which creative writers have a knack for helping the inner child in the search for identity. In *Steppenwolf* and *Siddhartha* by Herman Hesse, he shows a dual-natured character struggling between his bourgeois roots and his animal nature. Jack Kerouac's *On the Road* provided a picaresque (road story) version of how we sometimes need to do something to radically change our lives and also gain a new perspective. The wolf is the perfect symbol of the stage Erikson has outlined as Intimacy versus Isolation. In the book the animal part of Steppenwolf's nature is isolated while as we know in real life, wolves are herd or pack animals that have a well-established hierarchy. Hence, the idiom "lone wolf" is a misnomer in nature, but not in literature. The identity issue in Steppenwolf is one of intimacy versus isolation, illustrated in Eric Erikson's developmental schema which appears later in this book.

Then, there are particular issues by which creating scenes in fiction illuminate the issues of childhood in a dramatic way. One is illustrated by the Hemingway character Francis MacComber in "The Short Happy Life of Francis MacComber. This story is a classic example of the theme of sexual paranoia or jealousy. The issue of jealousy is the result of some type of childhood abandonment, either emotional or physical. In this case not so much in the character as in the author himself. In the story Francis has not lived up to the Hemingway code of grace under pressure. Instead of killing the lion, he has bolted and run, requiring that his guide, Wilson, shoot the animal instead. This is an irrevocable breach of his manhood. His wife sleeps with the guide, after having been completely shamed by Francis' cowardice and loss of face. The next day, the wife, while finally "turned on" by the excitement of killing, shoots Francis in the back of the head as he is about to reclaim his manhood. Francis is portrayed as an upper class husband who married someone who controlled him sexually and socially. The only control he has is his money, which in the framework of this story, is meaningless because Francis has no grace under pressure. The lion is the ultimate test of manhood in Hemingway's world, and it is better to stand and be eaten, than to fail this test. The loss of courage in Hemingway is the theme that arises from his family of origin, and the suicide of his father.

Inner Dialogue and Depression

Inner dialogue can be thought of as originating from the words and behavior of the parents toward their child. Think of it as being taped by the child from the time he or she begins to understand language. That is one example of the relationship between inner dialog and depression. David Burns in the *Feeling Good Handbook* 1989 discusses the interaction between thoughts and feelings and the role that this inner self talk plays in depression. In my view these inner dialogs arise out of real input absorbed by each of us as we develop within whatever family scenes we grew up with. Inner dialog is so powerful because the child was taping all messages send his or her way without any defenses to keep out the negative or abusive material.

In the case of someone who has come to therapy, these are usually painful messages which were absorbed by the child when he or she was too defenseless to reject or counteract the verbiage used by parents, parents who themselves were struggling with self-talk which came from their parents. As Janov and Harris make clear, the negative content is not necessarily the fault of the parents per se, it can be the result of the human condition of childhood. The client has usually lost the ability to be himself because he or she is in the process of trying to repeat the compulsions from the family of origin. Freud called this the repetition compulsion and "the destiny compulsion" (Berne, 58) in which the family script has a firm hold on clients with "losing" scripts.

Berne's description of the ego states of Parent, Adult, and Child are demonstrated in the auditory aspect of the psyche. "The Child expresses his wishes in visual images; but what he does about them, the final display through the final common pathway, is determined by auditory images, or voices in the head, the result of a mental dialog" (Berne, p. 369) Since the final common pathway of the patient's behavior is determined by voices in the head, this can be changed by getting another voice into his head, that of the therapist or that of a powerful character portrayed in a work of fiction. Through writing and therapy the therapist begins to hear the voices in a patient's head very quickly and accurately, usually before the patient can hear them herself.

"With some encouragement, the patient soon becomes aware of his or her most important script directives as spoken in his head, and can report them to the therapist. The therapist must then give the client the option of choosing between them, discarding the nonadaptive, useless, harmful, or misleading ones, and keeping the adaptive or useful ones. He may enable the client to get a friendly divorce from his parents and make a fresh start altogether. The therapist must give the client permission to disobey the Parental directives, not in rebellion but rather in autonomy" (Berne, p. 370).

The writing exercises in this book have helped to expose negative inner dialog through the act of putting it on paper. Most disruptive self talk comes from the Adapted Child (compliant or rebellious) and needs to be dealt with before any of us can change. As we expose the dark side of the inner child, we begin to make the two halves of our personalities familiar to each other.

In writing the problem is this: We produce 50,000 thoughts a day during our waking hours. This boils down to a least one thought per second per waking hour. What thoughts and feelings are the most important to record? This is where free writing, journaling, writing poetry, fiction, sketches, a novel, a play, or responding to an assignment will help the client first tune in to his or her own inner dialog, voices in the head, skull-rapping, or more commonly known as "self talk." Writers learn to train themselves to catch only the best self-talk as it rushes by them.

Look at it this way: About 40% of the Nobel Prize winning poets have been diagnosed with Major Depressive Disorder, Recurrent, or Bipolar I Disorder as they're called in the *DSM IV*. Writers have found a way to sift through these 50,000 inner messages and journaled, made poems or works of fiction and non-fiction which the rest of us can enjoy.

There are many ways to do this, but each writer must find his or her method for doing this. Faulkner and Truman Capote stayed up late with a bottle of whiskey and composed after the sun went down. Hemingway's inner Child was most active and open in the morning after waking, and he would reread everything he had written until he came to the blank page on his typewriter, writing until he knew what was going to happen next, and then he stopped. Some write all the time. James Thurber's wife would catch him composing as they were standing together at a cocktail party. "Stop writing

Thurber," she would say, "stop writing."

Some writers need yellow legal pads on which to compose; then they take the pads to a secretary or transcriber to be typed, reproducing the organic feel begun in childhood of putting words directly on paper with the hand. Some contemporary writers have a staff which they gather every morning to check the progress of the ideas which the author has told them to compose in the style of the author's previous books. There are those who use tape recorders in the car and by the bed to capture their ideas.

There is a great deal of childhood joy in participating in these creative writing rituals, which grow up around the capturing of one's self talk. For me it was always important to find a coffee shop wherein I could watch people and write but not have to talk to anyone. After an hour of journal writing I would remember my dreams and write those down as well. There was a relationship between the journal and the current project I was working on because the journal material was completely free writing and uncensored, and the project after the first draft was always goal oriented and focused around creating a potentially publishable work. But sometimes a new character would crawl out of the journal and sometimes the project writing would show up there with a problem or plot quandary to solve.

I would like to solve the problem some day, underlining the relationship between "self talk" and "hearing voices" or the hallucinations of schizophrenic humans who are plagued by their internal skull rapping, which seems to them to be coming from the outside. There were times in my youth when my inner dialog was overwhelming. I had one acid trip when I understood that the negative voices from my childhood revolved around the issue of feeling that I didn't belong anywhere. Pot, peyote, and mescaline all unleashed negative dialog for the entire duration of the drug's journey through my body. Valium, Darvon, Percoset, Seconal, Opiates and other pain-killing or muscle-relaxing medications seemed to make me "the human being I was meant to be." That person was the human being without anxiety. As I sit here writing on the computer and looking out my back yard, I am thankful that the desire to remain balanced inside of my psyche was more important than doing whatever it took to quiet my inner dialog.

Writing helps to uncover and confront issues which reside in the unconscious or past experiences, i.e. Inner Child, so that when they surface in the present, we already have some experience dealing with them. This also helps with our depression.

Most inner dialog can be thought of as a transcript which is taped from the minute the child is born until he or she is old enough to have awareness of the contradictions of parents, usually from 14 onward. Penfield's brain experiments with epileptic patients, in which he severed the corpus calosum to stop the seizures, revealed that with a mild electric probe, specific memories of clients could be accessed in various parts of the brain. The clients were awake during these experiments, sitting in a chair, and when the probe was applied they would literally be "playing hide and go seek in the back yard, listening to mother calling them to dinner, the smell of grass stains and loam fresh in their nostrils" (Harris, Introduction).

Creative writing works with depression no matter what type of counselor is using it. Writing affects both the left and right sides of the brain, according to most research, so structured and unstructured therapists both can benefit. Two types of counselors appear to be practicing therapy in the millennium: Those who believe they can change your behavior if you change the way you think, or those who believe they can change your behavior if you change the way you feel. I personally am in the latter group because feelings come out of the first seven years of childhood, and they are like a fire in each of us which burns from the fuel of our early vulnerability, smoldering in the center of our adult lives.

In my experience this is where the real change occurs when clients connect on the behaviors which repeat childhood feelings, patterns or decisions. The cognitive (change your thoughts) approach may work on specific issues in the short term, but feeling process therapies are more effective in the long term. The problem is we no longer have time nor money to spend on this type of counseling.

Now, in the Millennium, I see mental health professionals have lost some ground. We need to start over in teaching the public concerning the changes that have taken place in our field. At least in the 70s and 80s we had Woody Allen movies, which told of the long process of Psychoanalysis for millions of viewers. Now, that model is no longer in vogue. In place now are solution-focused and short- term interactions which help clients come to grips with current issues in their lives. There some mass media examples of how counseling therapy has evolved, "2 1/2 Men and The Sopranos", I hope this work will begin that process, especially by illustrating how creative writing is a vital part of the therapeutic process, and how creative writing can move the client further along in the process of counseling, by providing a record of thoughts, feelings and behaviors which occur when the client is away from the therapist.

The Surgeon General's Report on Mental Health in 2000 says that "more than 50 million Americans suffer from mental illness each year, and many fail to get treatment even when effective therapies are widely available." This is the first Surgeon General's report on mental health. Further on in Mark Kaufman's article in the Washington Post Donna Shalala says the report documents that "Today, mental illness is the second-leading cause of disability, the second-leading cause of premature death in the United States."

According to Kaufman, 20 percent of Americans are believed to experience a mental disorder each year. As I write this in 2009 with 300 million Americans, that would mean that 60 million Americans will suffer from mental illness this year. It's also astounding that under President Clinton, this is the first report since 1964 to address mental health. Further, most estimates of the most serious mental disorders, Schizophrenia and Bipolar I Disorder, conclude that 1% of the population will develop the former and 1% will develop the latter. That means that six million Americans with these two disorders alone will require medications and therapy throughout their entire life spans.

I am concerned that people who need help seem to have no concept of what therapy or counseling are. There were many movies produced in the 60s and 70s which portrayed some of the processes of therapy, such as Cuckoo's Nest, Manhattan, I Never Promised You a Rose Garden, and Ordinary People. Clients now need some education concerning the strengths and limitations of counseling. If I look back at the counselors I've had, it's quite a spectrum of styles and personalities. The single most important thread running through all counseling is getting in touch with feelings and expressing them appropriately in daily life, especially anger. Dr. David Viscott states, "All unexpressed anger ends with a client or individual in "emotional bankruptcy."

The importance of writing is increased in the current climate in which many insurance companies do not cover mental health benefits at all. Clients may be limited to five or six visits a year and may have a high deductible or copay, making it impossible for them to come on any regular basis. Through the use of writing with these clients, some kind of continuity can be maintained during the weeks or months a client is away from the counselor.

It was Arthur Janov's view that primal or feeling process therapy with neurotics involved shredding the unreal self by invoking the client's major "primal scene" and working through the mental and physical pain of those scenes, which lodge in the body and memory. Primal scenes are gut-grabbing incidents in fiction, poetry and movies. Take for example the rape scene in Prince of Tides. The primal scene is the culmination of many other "scenes" in one's life which are epitomized by the incident which solidifies or freezes the defenses permanently in a child's psyche. Nick Nolte's character remembers a gang rape perpetrated upon his sister, but he doesn't remember that he too was raped during that scene. The Barbara Streisand character is the psychoanalyst treating Nolte's sister, and the scene is depicted in the movie as a flashback, much the same way he would experience it in therapy or in nightmares.

Creative writing, when used in the context of psychodynamic therapy, can assist clients in tracing the trail of "crumbs" back through the forest of their childhoods because it stimulates memory. I have had many clients who say, "I can't remember anything from first grade to sixth grade" because they have blocked off their trauma, but when they start journaling or doing the writing exercises, the memories start to surface.

When people begin writing, they first notice how vulnerable they are, almost from the first word. Writing is an act of exposure which brings the exposure to light in a semi-permanent way.

There are three ways to communicate: verbal, physical, and written. Writing is then crucial to the treatment of most clients who have problems communicating. Writing also helps maintain continuity in therapy from one session to the next, and it can be used to help a client continue working after therapy has terminated. "Writing can be a wound turned to light," I contend, paraphrasing Jacques Braque.

The most prevalent types of writing people do when they are in therapy include journaling, letter writing, poetry, sketches, childhood memories, notebooks, dream journals, dialogs, personal ads, and free writing.

Free writing evolved from the psychological process of free association used by Freud with his clients at the beginning of psychoanalysis. Clients who are terrified of letting others know how they feel, can start with these fragmented forms and first reveal to themselves their true thoughts and feelings; then, they can later dialog them out loud to the therapist and eventually learn what it is they must say to the people in their lives. I call these practices "rehearsals," as if the client is rehearsing what to say to significant others.

Here then, are creative writing assignments I have used with hundreds of my clients during the past ten years of being a Licensed Clinical Social Worker. Some of these are standard with most clients; others are highly unusual and need to be directed at clients whom the therapist knows will specifically benefit from the assignment.

Interactive Creative Writing Exercises and Schizophrenia

As I began to focus on writing exercises for people who have schizophrenia, I thought of the novelist Kurt Vonnegut, who has publicly discussed his schizophrenia, and a relative of mine who is an excellent poet. I mention this simply to remind myself and others how a mental health diagnosis doesn't necessarily restrict the accomplishments of the person who has it! According to the *DSM-IV-TR* (2000, p. 153) the following symptoms characterize people with schizophrenia: (1) delusions (2) hallucinations (3) disorganized speech (frequent derailment or incoherence) (4) grossly disorganized or catatonic behavior 5) negative symptoms, i.e. flat affect (feelings), alogia or avolition. Only one symptom is required if delusions are bizarre or hallucinations consist of a voice or voices keeping up a running commentary on the person's behavior or thoughts, or two or more voices conversing with each other.

Most research has shown that schizophrenics benefit primarily from milieu therapy that is support from their families, group therapy, and vocational rehabilitation. However, many also receive counseling and psychosocial rehabilitation in many states, and with these support services, often manage to stay out of psychiatric hospitals for long periods of time.

In general, a schizophrenic's first episode of decompensation or psychotic "break" occurs during adolescence or late adolescence, but I have found during many psychiatric assessments at an in-patient facility that children are often aware of their voices much earlier, as young as six years old. During this psychotic episode, of course, writing is not an effective treatment tool, and if the client is writing during this time, it often entails documenting the content of disturbing hallucinations or delusions, such as being followed, poisoned, infected, loved at a distance, deceived by spouse or lover, or having a disease.

During the recovery phase, clients can begin to return to their lives outside the hospital. Continuing medications is the most important behavior which must be followed if the schizophrenic is to successfully reintegrate into his or her daily life. Even the current crop of atypical anti-psychotic medications has bothersome side effects, and you can understand how that would feed into the delusion of being poisoned.

The newest ones are significantly "cleaner," and those include Abilify, Geodon, Risperdal, and others. Once a schizophrenic person is stabilized on meds, he or she can begin using writing exercises to some degree as a tool to maintain mental health. Let's begin with a worksheet which helps the client describe his or her own symptoms that family can watch for if their family member is on a downward spiral.

Symptoms of a downward spiral is based on "Schizophrenia: A Handbook for Families" by Health Canada, 1997. If the writing assignment is used during the downward spiral, its best if the person just fills in the blanks rather than trying to originate coherent sentences, since that's one of the symptoms.

ARE YOU EXPERIENCING RELAPSE SYMPTOMS DURING THE PAST TWO TO FOUR WEEKS?

1. I have no interest in doing things._____

2. I don't bathe or change clothes._____

3. My residence is messy._____

4. I can't concentrate or think straight._____

5. I have racing thoughts._____

6. I am withdrawing from people, including family._____

7. I have stopped taking my medications._____

8. I can't make decisions._____

9. I have disturbing thoughts._____

10. I can't sleep._____

11. I feel bad, tense, and worthless for no reason._____

12. I'm not eating._____

13. I smoke continually._____

14. People are talking about me._____

15. I talk but don't make sense._____

16. I have bad dreams._____

17. I am too pushy or argue too much._____

18. I have thoughts of hurting or killing myself._____

19. I have thoughts of hurting or killing others._____

20. I'm using street drugs._____

(I discovered in therapy that some clients use meth to eradicate hallucinations temporarily.)_____

21. Parts of my body are changing or different._____

22. My surroundings are strange or unreal._____

23. I sleep a lot._____

24. People say I look or act differently._____

25. I am having sexual thoughts._____

26. I feel frightened in formerly comfortable situations._____

27. Others don't care about me._____

28. Others are trying to hurt or poison me._____

29. I experience other feelings or sensations:_____

People with schizophrenia can create writing both positive and negative. The Unabomber, for example, insisted on having his delusional tract published in the paper before he turned himself in. Others are capable of poetry, fiction (Kurt Vonnegut), non-fiction, and journalism. Daniel B. Fisher, himself a recovering schizophrenic, writes about his recovery from the disorder in the *Washington Post*, 2001, citing a study by Courtenay Harding which found that two-thirds of schizophrenics were living and functioning independently, and that half were medication free thirty years later.

Clients can write or focus their symptom review on the five indicators taken from the DSM-IV, 2000.

1. Today I experienced delusions, scale of 0-5:_____

2. Today I had hallucinations (voices, visual):_____

3. Today I had trouble speaking, I had derailed thoughts:_____

4. Today I was badly disorganized or catatonic:_____

5. Today I have blunted feelings, no logic, and no desire to live:_____

Managing Voices

The following is based on a worksheet called "Voice Management Guidelines" by Larry E. Banta, M.D., distributed at West Valley Medical Center's closed psychiatric unit, Caldwell, Idaho. Hearing voices is a major symptom of schizophrenia, and it's oftentimes made fun of in comedy routines, on TV, in movies, and in fiction. I ask all of my clients about the type of voices, the number of voices, and the content of the dialog which the voices convey to the schizophrenic/s brain.

According to Banta, "Voices are caused by chemical imbalances in the auditory cortex of the brain, allowing the part of the brain that deals with the sense of hearing, to create its own stimulus from memories or even creating new voices that have nothing to do with any memories. Sometimes the voices actually cause the person's own voice and mouth to create the sound that is heard. These are called subvocalizations."

Most recently, a client said that his voices constituted a roomful of people, all talking about him. With his medication, the volume of these voices became a murmur during which he could not make out the content. When his meds needed adjusting or he had stopped taking them, the sound in his head was unbearable, and caused him to be forced to focus on the negative things they were saying about him. In other words, imagine a roomful of people standing around saying negative things about you! What a party!

Another client heard the Devil and Jesus arguing over the worthiness of his body and soul to continue living after he could not afford to pay for his Clonodine. To relieve the stress from this debate, he tried to throw himself out a Plexiglas window from a second story to end this dialog. I used to believe that illegal drugs would only serve to increase the level of the voices, but another client who was schizophrenic and a meth addict said that while he was high, the meth silenced his voices for the two or three days he was high.

You can see from these examples that writing exercises with schizophrenic clients should be done only when the client has stabilized on medications and is functioning at a reasonable cognitive level.

Guidelines for managing voices:

1. Rate the voices at a level from 0 to 10, ten being the worst and zero being absent._____

2. Use this rating to talk with your doctor, so he or she will know how severe the problem is._____

3. Know that stress and emotions can make the voices worse. Work with your doctor or therapist to know when you may need a medication adjustment._____
_____

4. A journal may be helpful to connect on when the voices are at their worst and what might be making them worse. Sometimes a noisy or confusing environment, a loud radio or TV, or the opposite, a place that's too quiet like a library. Often, the screaming, squealing and yelling of children can cause clients to hear voices. Write down the times when voices increase or become negative or suicidal._____
_____
_____

5. When the voices are bad, you might be helped by one of the following techniques:
   - Use a walkman or stereo headphones with relaxing, instrumental music, either New Age or Classical.
   - Humming or whistling which will take care of the subvocalizations.
   - Restricting environmental stimulus, i.e. go to a quiet, safe place.
   - Put on a book on tape. It could be a novel, biography or self-help book.
   - Change your activity. If you are sitting at home, take a walk, if you're busy with a project, take a breather and do something else for a short period. It you're watching TV or listening to the radio, you do something quiet for a while.

Most of the research I have seen during the past 15 years indicates that group therapy or day treatment programs are the most effective means of treatment, not individual psychotherapy per se. Once the individual has a psychiatrist, case management, and is connected to a social treatment milieu, he or she is then only limited by the degree of functioning and preparation that has already taken place in their lives.

If that individual writes on his or her own, then many of the following exercises in CWFC may be shared, as long as the counselor knows the particular issues which may give the person problems if he or she tries to write about them. I have been surprised by what clients are capable of, even while recovering from an episode in the hospital.

One important resource for clients with schizophrenia is the movie *A Beautiful Mind*, starring Russell Crowe. In it, the director of the movie was able to visually show the disabling effect of the hallucinations that the main character was having. This movie also helps audiences to understand that people with this disorder also have strengths and talents they can give to the world.

Bipolar Disorder

Bipolar disorder is a severe biological disorder that affects about 1.2% of the adult population in the United States, more than 3.6 million. *Time* magazine in a recent article reports that not only are the numbers of individuals with bipolar increasing, but also it 's affecting younger and younger people, including children as young as six years old. Mood disorders are "biological illnesses that affect our ability to experience normal mood states." They are treatable medical illnesses which are caused by changes in brain chemistry.

In a manic episode these symptoms are present for a minimum of one week and make it very difficult for the person to function: Feeling unusually high, euphoric, or irritable, needing little sleep, yet having great amounts of energy, pressured speech, racing thoughts, easily distracted, having an inflated feeling of power, grandiosity, greatness or importance, doing reckless things without concern about possible bad consequences, bad investments, inappropriate sexual activity, no impulse control.

Bipolar depressions are some of the most severe in the mental health field. In a major depressive episode, these symptoms are present for at least two weeks and make it difficult for the person to function: Feeling hopeless, losing interest in the things one usually enjoys, difficulty sleeping or sleeping too much, extremes in appetite, problems concentrating and making decisions, feeling slowed down or agitated, feeling worthless or guilty, low self-esteem, thoughts of suicide or death.

During my supervisory training, I once asked my supervisor what should be done with a person in therapy who is diagnosed bipolar? She answered, the same as everybody else, as long as that person is on medications! However, bipolar people also typically possess above average intelligence, and hence many writers, musicians, actors, and artists have been diagnosed with bipolar I disorder, including Ben Stiller, Patti Duke, Carrie Fisher, Thomas Wolfe, Jackson Pollock, Charlie Parker, Danny Bonaduce, Dick Cavett, Francis Ford Coppola, Robert Downey Jr., Carrie Fisher, Margot Kidder, Tony Orlando, Jimmie Piersall, Darryl Strawberry, Brian Wilson of the Beach boys, and Jonathan Winters, and countless others.

I am convinced that a Bipolar I person who is having a manic episode, may be experiencing something similar to an epileptic seizure because his or her brain is undergoing a milder electrical storm. Many of the newer mood stabilizers, such as Depakote, Tegretol and Triliptal are actually anti-seizure medications, which researchers discovered also work for people with Bipolar I Disorder.

According to the *PDR Drug Guide for Mental Health Counselors*, there are 35,000 physicians in psychiatric practice, 70,000 psychologists, 200,000 social workers, and 50,000 marriage and family therapists, a total of 355,000 practitioners (p. v). Plus, there are thousands of Psychosocial Rehabilitation counselors, drug and alcohol facilitators, case managers, Psychiatric Nurses, Psychiatric Technicians, and school counselors who work at every school and university in the nation.

During the past 15 years of practicing therapy, I have work with many teenagers who have been diagnosed with Bipolar I Disorder, (henceforth known as bipolar) and one common thread among them is that journaling is a popular and therapeutic way of helping them deal with racing thoughts and pressured speech. During either manic or depressive episodes, journaling helps relieving that pressure, and clients who kept journals are asked to bring them in to their sessions if they feel comfortable sharing.

Mary Ann Reuter writes, "Personal Journaling has become so popular that Writer's Digest Books has introduced a magazine called Personal Journaling: Writing About Your Life" (Treasure Valley Fifty-Plus Living, p. 6). Journaling is a crucial therapeutic tool for clients to discover their inner dialog, to enhance their communication with others, and to explore issues in their lives. For some, combining writing with creating a scrapbook or a photo album collects several media together in one place and helps prompts positive and negative memories during the process of therapy. Reuter also notes that journals help explore inner creativity… remember dreams…explore the deeper self…document a spiritual journey…experience psychological release… defuse feelings…recognize emotional trends over time.

There were several important models for me when I began to keep a journal. The first was *Notebooks* by Albert Camus. The others included *Letters to Theo* by Vincent Van Gogh, and *Anais Nin's Diaries*. There are many others, but those I read during my formative years as a writer, giving me excellent models of what journaling could be. Nearly every important idea or project I completed "crawled" out of my journal and grew on its own after leaving the pages of my journal. Now, I have 30 journals, notebooks, diaries, spanning 41 years of my life from 1963 until 2005.

In therapy, there are several basic journal entries that clients can use over and over again as they write to get in touch with their feelings and thoughts (*The Feeling Process: A Workbook for Men* by Steve Flick):

1) Free association
2) Inner dialog or "skull-rapping"
3) Outer dialog or "eavesdropping"
4) Thoughts, feelings and issues of their daily lives
5) Reflecting on the events going on around them, reading they are doing, their counseling or therapy
6) Childhood memories
7) Descriptions of people
8) Descriptions of places
9) Primal scenes
10) Write your dreams.

BASIC JOURNAL ENTRIES FOR SELF-DISCOVERY AND GROWTH AS A WRITER

James Pennebaker at the University of Texas has found that journaling for 20 minutes, three days a week can lower blood pressure, reduce missed workdays, increase immunity, and reduce visits to the doctor (Sonia Haller, *The Arizona Republic*).

I am astounded that someone has studied journaling for twenty years, and secondly, I am thankful that there has been research which supports the value of keeping a journal. I have kept a journal for almost 45 years, and it is the source for all of my writing projects and has become the way I process information in my life. From my experience with my own journal and study of other journal types, here are the primary entries clients can be taught to use a journal. The most important model for my journaling came from Albert Camus' *Notebooks* in which Camus revealed the way his ideas and feelings metamorphosed into his fiction and philosophy.

Do a free writing by putting on some instrumental music (lyrics get in the left brain and prevent concentration). This form comes from Ken McCrorie's book *Telling Writing*. Once you sit down to free write and place your pen on paper, you don't remove the pen. Write without worrying about spelling, punctuation, grammar, or organization since the idea is to capture as many of your thoughts and feelings as you can. If you can't think of anything to write, you write "I can't think of anything to write" until something comes. Another one I developed from my time in the classroom can lets you write what's happening right around you at the moment, or lets you write about when you got up this morning and write your way into the present. After about ten or fifteen minutes, stop and read your free writing. Pick one unusual sentence and circle it. This technique is what every writer does nearly every day of his or her life, whether it be in a journal, notebook, computer, laptop, letter, or paper napkin.

_____
_____
_____
_____
_____
_____
_____

Write a dream that you had or a dream that repeats on a consistent basis. If you can't remember one, put this workbook by the bed and tell yourself you're going to remember your dream tonight when you wake up. Research on sleep has shown that we dream every night, it's just that many times we don't remember the dreams. For a week or two, go to a coffee shop or restaurant before going to work. Sit down and do a free writing. Some time during the two weeks you will remember one or more of your dreams. Focus on the events in the dream and the feelings which accompany it.

_____
_____
_____
_____
_____
_____

Write some inner dialog which is the brain's response to feelings. Cognitive therapists call this "self talk," and it's important to tell the truth about your self talk. Voices in the head, mental dialog, auditory images come from actual words you heard as a child from parents or other caretakers. Negative inner dialog can prevent you from making progress in life. Look at some bits of inner speak you have concerning your body, your relationships, money, your job, and your self esteem.

_____
_____
_____
_____
_____

Creative Writing for Counselors and Their Clients - Steve Flick M.F.A., LCSW

Eavesdrop on outer dialog, conversations outside of yourself. Sit on a bench at the mall, in a college cafeteria, at an airport, and collect snippets of conversation which you hear around you. It's amazing what people say to each other in public places. In my favorite Winchell's doughnut shop in San Jose the patrons were business people, college students, and street people. The words which got through my own anxiety, helped provide a window for me into understanding the problems and goals of other people.

___

Describe a person that you know well, by having them do a "sitting," much as a painter would have a model sit quietly to reflect the body language and look outward into the essence of another person. This exercise requires that you use a thesaurus, so that you can expand your ability to describe. It helped me understand how to expand my ability to render things visually, instead of simply reporting the "skull-rapping" in my overwrought brain. Start from the hair. Use concrete descriptive words, not emotional or value-laden words. Use simple sentences, using present tense verbs, focusing on the color, shape, movement, and effect of the hair on the face. Move to the forehead...the nose...eyes, eyebrows, cheekbones, lips, chin and coloring. Notice that everything has a shape, color, and relationship to the whole. Describe the shoulders, stomach, hips, thighs, calves and feet. Include any clothing the person is wearing. Make it a goal to exhaustively report everything you see. Then, and only then summarize the effect of the person's physical presence on you.

Creative Writing for Counselors and Their Clients - Steve Flick M.F.A., LCSW

Describe a place using the thesaurus again and adopting the same approach. Sit in a park, your back yard, a campus, downtown, and "frame" the area you are going to include with your hands. Start from the left and include every shade of green you see on the particular tree or bush. Look at the words that are available for green, using concrete descriptive vocabulary. Use either specific color words, i.e. celadon, lime, turquoise, or use objects, which we are familiar with that possess the kind of green you want your reader to see. Remember still that everything has a shape, a color, a texture and sometimes movement. Make your way from left to right, top to bottom. Feel the fence under the trees with your hand and describe that. This exercise helps clients and writers move outside their own subjectivity into the outer world.

If this is too overwhelming, select a two-foot square of grass and do a "miniature" description of everything in the square. I need to credit Robert Pirsig in *Zen and the Art of Motorcycle Maintenance* for this one because he describes a young woman in his book who cannot focus on her paper until he tells that writing student to focus on "one brick in the building in her home town" and begin from there.

Write a childhood memory by using a scrapbook, photo album, video, home movies, or anything that triggers your recollection. Pretend that someone is performing a Penfield brain experiment on you, and that you have electrodes in your head which have extracted one scene for you to re-experience. In that scene, focus on the minute, sensual details of smell, taste, touch, hearing, sight. Remember the dialog and everything around you. Therapists can sometimes use relaxation and visualization techniques to assist clients in recovering childhood memories while they write.

Reflect on something you've read in the paper or in a book you're involved in. In the beginning my journals were full of other people's ideas and experiences, and the journal was the testing ground on which I rejected or absorbed the material I read. The books and articles we read become the "programming" of our psyches, so it's important that clients get their hands on the best information they can find.

Write about personal issues and conflicts you are going through. When I talk about this with other people, they always bring up the problem that they are afraid other people will find their journals and read them. The way clients write and verbalize their issues gives a therapist a starting point for helping clients take control of their lives. Journaling is the format through which I learned to say my feelings to the important people in my life. If you process your thoughts and feelings in a journal, there is always the chance that someone may find it, but the longer you keep it, the journal becomes the way you process your life. In most cases if you have left it somewhere, it's because you unconsciously want someone to share the material with anyway.

_____
_____
_____
_____
_____

The therapist has to remember that writing is reliving, and for some clients the act of writing brings back painful experiences which writing probes almost from the first sentence. Because the preceding exercises are not only therapeutic, they also are ways to help adolescents move their writing toward a more focused type of writing which may or may not turn into poems, songs, rap, short stories or novels. The other function of a journal is to examine feelings privately before they are communicated to others. Because feelings are distorted by the imbalances inherent in bipolar, the journal provides an intermediary stage for them to simmer and cool, allowing the writer to decide if they should be shared with the people in their lives.

People with bipolar disorder are tempted to stop taking their meds—they may feel free of symptoms and think they don't need it any more. They may find the side effects hard to deal with, or they may miss the "high" they experience during hypo manic episodes. Half of all those diagnosed with bipolar abuse alcohol or drugs during their illness, in an attempt to "self-medicate" symptoms. Nearly one of five bipolar individuals will die from suicide, making it one of the most lethal psychiatric illnesses. The journal will assist the counselor and individual in keeping track of suicidal ideation.

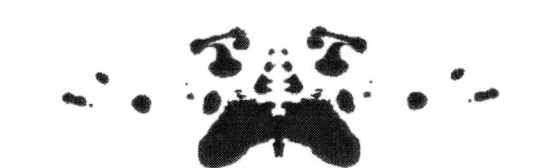

EXPAND YOUR JOURNAL WRITING WITH PROMPTS

These are some examples of "prompts" which help writers change the relationship to their material and unblock fragments of writing which lead them back to the well.

The entire 365 prompts can be seen online at www.writersdigest.com/writingprompts.asp or you can buy or see the December 12th, 2002 issue of *Writer's Digest*, page 19. Prompts help writers by focusing their thoughts on a particular problem, issue, poem or story they want to develop. Prompts help writers escape the subjectivity of their emotions and project into another entity.

Creative Writing for Counselors and Their Clients - Steve Flick M.F.A., LCSW

Solve a problem for a character in a piece you have been working on. _____

Whom would you like to talk to right now? _____

Write about a character who would like to return a gift but cannot. _____

_____

Write yourself a letter (on separate paper) to be opened one year from now. What goals do you hope to accomplish by then? What do you tell your future self about what's going on now?
Write about your first experience with death. Describe the people, the place, the event, the cemetery, the dialog, and the effect that person had on the people around him or her.

_____

_____

_____

Write a self portrait, describing yourself in detail. Start from the hair and work your way downward as if looking at a stranger.

_____

_____

_____

Write about your first experience with birth? Describe the moments before going to the hospital, the process of admittance, delivery, aftermath, and any dialog you remember.

_____

Create two or three characters from facets of your personality, i.e. your compulsive side, ADD side, angry side, and put them in a car driving to the coast.
Write about a lie you told.
Write a scene in which a character suffers a public moment. Take time to fully develop the scene and avoid exposition (narrative explanation.)
Fictionalize an idea based on a real event but don't stick to the facts, apply all of your own motivations and behaviors to the situation.
Write a story from a child's point of view; focus on language, dialog, perspective, and experience.

_____

Watch a movie halfway through; then, write two or three plausible endings and see which one is closest to the movie's ending.
Write a commencement speech that you will give to high school seniors graduating from your high school.

_____

Imagine a young married woman who is out with her girlfriends in a pickup bar. She calls her husband to leave a message, and instead of hanging up properly, the phone stays on. As she gets drunker, she begins to complain about her husband. Next, she responds to the advances of a young hustler and ends up going home with him. The purse is beside her everywhere she goes. (This one's mine, S.F.)

_____

Sit next to a popular booth in your favorite coffee shop. Practice "eavesdropping" on conversations of people who sit by you for at least two hours. Take notes and write out the dialogs on computer, including descriptions of the people and the place.
Write a story based on an event in your own life. Change the name of the main character and magnify the conflict.

_____

JOURNAL ON A PERSONAL AD

I use this exercise with singles and with men and women who are married and who still fantasize on having sex with other people. Its purpose is to help the clients realize that they are fantasizing and open up and share these thought dreams with their partners, or to help the client get in touch with what needs his or her partner is not fulfilling.

Open up your local newspaper or alternative paper and read through the personal ads. Allow yourself to pretend you are single and unattached if you're in a relationship now. If you're single, use this to help define what you want or think you want. Go to an Internet dating site and begin investigating ads that people write to describe themselves. With these as a model, begin writing your own.

What physical qualities are you looking for? Be completely honest about this. Then, define the psychological traits you consider to be important. Further, define the life stage you consider yourself to be in, so the person answering the ad could tell if you had something in common.

Are you single, divorced, widowed, or a single parent? What are your major interests in life? Are you working class, middle class, upper class, or wealthy? Do you find it hard to categorize yourself? Try it anyway and see what happens.

Write a personal ad without regard to length or cost. Describe what you're looking for. As you read through the ads, look for women (future partners) who describe themselves in a way that you like. "Classy petite blonde…shy black female…Cinderella seeks Prince, beautiful, talented PhD…sense of humor…" Write out all the characteristics which arouse your curiosity. Do religion, ethnic background, occupation, marital status, motherhood play a part in your selection process? By allowing yourself to write your wants, needs, fixations and dreams on paper, you can sometimes begin to sort through the discrepancy between appearances and reality in your sexual relationships and psychosocial life. Write the ads which turn you on the most or arouse your curiosity. Find several you would actually answer and write them here. Why did you choose the ones you did?

_____
_____
_____
_____
_____

If you examine the ads from a critical perspective, we can see that all or most of the negative qualities are omitted. Now, write an ad which asks for a woman who can deal with the difficult aspects of your life. For example: "Man who has child-support payments, visitation of young son, old car, who is satisfied by non-remunerative careers in music, teaching, writing and counseling, needs psychic space, likes to write, daydream and hoard his money. Would like to meet a financially independent woman who had a good relationship with her father, likes to shop at thrift stores, a tall brunette with good legs to share my life."

WRITE YOUR OWN AD, TELLING THE TRUTH ABOUT YOURSELF

_____
_____
_____

Analyze the difference between what you want and what you expect in a partner and the reality of your life. Do you expect too much from the woman or man of your dreams? Do you expect less of a partner than you do from yourself? The partner on the symbolic level, is the representation of the feminine or masculine qualities you have in your unconscious or "shadow" self (Carl Jung). In reality, the psychological qualities of femininity or masculinity we seek are simply a reflection of unmet needs from childhood. Once you begin to supply those needs to yourself, the partner is free to be with you as him or herself, not as the representation of unmet needs. What expectations do you have of partners that seem unrealistic, now that you've written your ad and looked at ads? What connections can you make between your relationships to your mother/father?

_____
_____
_____
_____
_____

BENEFITS AND DRAWBACKS OF JOURNALING

Keeping a journal is only a step in the therapeutic process. It is the first stage in a client's journey towards making external his or her internal dialog or "skull rapping." It's the first place one puts his or her feelings in the morning. After a period of keeping a journal, the client begins to see patterns in his or her behavior, thinking, feeling, and needs to take responsibility for them. Arthur Janov in *The Primal Scream* writes about the fact that writers symbolize their pain instead of feeling it, and they become great at symbolizing. The next step from journaling is communicating to a real person. That can be a therapist or a trusted friend. Often, this is a very difficult step for clients who grew up in households where expressing their feelings led to such commotion that as adults they believe that they will experience psychic "death" if they let someone know how they feel.

In my own case, I was unable to express my anger appropriately, and I kept seeing angry feelings in the journal, but no one knew how I felt because I couldn't tell them. Eventually, the pressure would build up, and I would leave the situation, that being my primary defense against expressing my feelings. Journaling is also extremely subjective. You haven't brought the feelings out yet in the process of reality testing, i.e. "Do you love me? Did I make you angry? You stabbed me in the back, why? I didn't get the raise? Why did you sleep with someone else?" Therefore there is a vital stage after journaling wherein the client has to make public the feelings to the people in his or her life. This is the part that takes support and sometimes therapy.

Carl Jung, the psychotherapist, told James Joyce after Joyce was told that his daughter was schizophrenic, "Mr. Joyce, you float to the bottom of the sea of language, but your daughter is sinking." All writers come to a point where they want to move from journal writing to poetry, stories, novels, scripts, or creative non-fiction, i.e. New Journalism. Some clients are sinking to the bottom of language, and some are floating. If you client is the latter, it's okay to assign him or her writing assignments to be done as homework. In the former, sometimes writing is a part of a delusional system, say you client feels the FBI is watching him and he needs to put all of his secrets in writing before he is killed, it would not help that client to do a lot of writing.

POETRY AS THERAPEUTIC RELEASE

"I write poetry to heal myself" Author Unknown. Alan Ginsberg opens the PBS Video *Walt Whitman* by saying, "I slept with someone who slept with Walt Whitman!" In some respects his is the human response to the generativity of poetry and writing to an audience, which is to be loved and accepted in mind and in body. Over and over again I have heard musicians say that they began playing the guitar so that they could "get girls." Why a poet or writer would deny that, at least in his or her youth, he or she began writing to get the attention of the sex to which they were attracted. Ginsberg's mother was schizophrenic and suffered many breakdowns during his childhood. Ginsberg himself was a patient in the Columbia Psychiatric Institute in 1949, according to *The Norton Anthology of American Literature*, volume 2, 1994. Consequently, the contribution of Ginsberg is much like the journal made public without the "pretense of poetry." The pretense was mostly based on speaking frankly and in graphic terms to his audience. It is also the cry of the abandoned child counteracting the madness in his mother and himself. "I saw the best minds of my generation destroyed by madness, starving hysterical naked, dragging themselves through the Negro streets at dawn looking for an angry fix."

Much of modern poetry arises out of the journaling process. Journaling is an important stage in the process of self-expression. Aside from academic poetry, there is also a movement from the streets which involves the "Poetry Slam," a competitive, sometimes wholly improvised, sometimes written down group experience which focuses on the poet's verbal expression more than on the power of his or her process of revision and contemplation of each poem.

A favorite exercise of mine comes from Peter Elbow's book *Writing With Power* (1981) and involves techniques from Elbow's chapter titled "Poetry as No Big Deal." This one is particularly successful with young bipolar and/or depressed young men and women who are journaling furiously and need some direction for the raw, untamed inner dialog that is pouring out of them. Here are some examples for journal entries that can grow into poems (Elbow, 1981).

Creative Writing for Counselors and Their Clients - Steve Flick M.F.A., LCSW

Begin each line with "I wish." _____

Begin each line with "once." _____

Begin each line with "I remember." _____

Begin each line with a color. _____

Begin each line with a Spanish word, a part of the body, a country, weather, a season, a book, an animal, and end with a smell. _____

Describe a room. _____

Start the poem with a swear word. _____

Start the poem with someone's actual speech. _____

Start the poem as a letter to a real person. _____

Write to the demon you feel you are struggling with. _____

Take all of these starter techniques and jumble them all up together. _____

Here is a starter technique for beginning a poem, which is not threatening, yet it allows readers to become writers, critics, and to begin creating their own poetry. It's called a "substitution" poem. Fill in your own choice of words, either by imitating the sound and sense of the original poem, or by following the directions under the omitted word. The real poem is by James Wright called "*This is What I Wanted*." Read it first out loud; then, write your own version.

THE ORIGINAL
*Today I was so happy, so I made this poem
As the plump squirrel scampers
Across the roof of the corncrib,
The moon suddenly stands up in the darkness,
And I see it is impossible to die.
Each moment of time is a mountain
An eagle rejoices in the oak trees of heaven,
Crying
This is (is not) what I wanted.*

Now, write your version by filling in the blanks.

Today I was so (mood) _____ so I (verb) _____ this (noun) _____

As the (adjective) _____ (animal) _____ (verb) _____

(prepositional phrase) _____ the (noun) _____ of the (noun) _____

The (noun) _____ (adverb) _____ stands up in the darkness,

And I see that it is impossible to (verb) _____.

Each moment of time is a (noun) _____.

A (noun) _____ (verb) _____ in the (noun) _____

of (place) _____

_____ (ing)

THIS IS (IS NOT) WHAT I WANTED.

25

Another type of substitution involves the creation of a structure which allows the client to fill in his or her own emotions without having to worry about what format to use or how to express them. This particular format was used with an 11-year-old boy whose parents had just separated and were in counseling, but were thinking about divorce.

When JT was born in_____, his dad had remarried_____, and she had a daughter named_____. She had a "first" dad named _____. This type is family can be called_____.
Now dad and your mom_____ are thinking they can't_____ _____anymore. Do you think this is your fault?_____? Don't worry, all kids think that. The hardest part about divorce or separation for you is_____ _____. When you first learned about this where were you? _____. (Don't forget mad, sad, glad, scared). Have you read Dinosaur's Divorce? _____. There may be new people in the lives of your mom and dad.
Dad is different because _____.
Mom is different because_____ . I can tell my feelings to _____right now. I can't talk to_____right now. Some good things can come when the adults _____. Make a list of three good things that have come out of this: 1

POETRY FROM A DEPRESSED TEENAGED GIRL

In this next example, a young client of 15 (Jessica S.) has written poetry about her relationship with a young man who was her first sexual partner. It's obvious the boy is using the main character, Lily, because he never calls, talks, or socializes with the protagonist, except to have sex on the campus of the school. There are several issues raised in the story, which were concurrent with J's therapy, including what her friends thought of her, dealing with another boy who was interested in her, some organic depression, an active intelligence, and advanced verbal skills. Plus, her parents were locked into a loveless, non-interactive marriage.

Jessica had a diagnosis of Major Depressive Disorder, Recurrent, and began a course of Zoloft after she told me she had tried to overdose on Ibuprofen during her third therapy session. She was involved with a young boy who was making her have sex on the school campus where they both went.

Going Forward

A heart cannot be broken so selfishly for you.
You break it and my heart shatters into a million pieces.
Love just isn't a word to speak to one you think you will
Love forever more.
The soul cannot be given up so easily or thrown away
Without a care.
Love cannot live without the other.
Passion cannot be ignited without a spark and or the flame.
Misery cannot love company.
Chocolate cannot be better than you.
Ice cream (raspberry) cannot be as good as the love you
Bring to me.
Heartache cannot be as painful as it seems.
Losing you cannot drive me out of my mind.
Then yes, the heart will become broken some way or
Another.
Someplace, somewhere heartache will catch up with you.
Losing someone brings you onto the brink of insanity.
Love is just a word that can be said again and again, though
Not true.
Misery does love company.
Passion can be flown through your veins without the other to
Spark the flame.
I find that chocolate is better than love.
Ice cream is better than what you give me, and what you
Think I want.
The soul is given up to you so many times.
Pain and regret is the aftermath of what love is, and there is
No turning back, only forward.

FALLING IN LOVE WITH YOU

Love is the poison that hides behind the heartbreak.
Desire holds the key to forever with you here in my arms.
Lust plays this game that neither one of us can win.
Passion sees a love that will never have the flame.
Whispers in the darkness can not hear the truth.
Dreams you and I dream will never come true.
Arms could never reach far enough to comfort the tears.
Secrets we never tell are as the lies that kill our love.
Dancing won't be the same once you are no longer here.
Eternity cannot be forever if forever was not eternity.
Power that lights the spark of bliss is never felt nor held.
Oblivious would not make me tremble as I hold you near.
Moonlight blinds the taker of unconditional things.
Pleasure and pain were not the freedom unto a heart.
Innocence won't be broken or so these lovers say.
Stars in the night sky glitter with glee for no reason.
Laughter is never the best medicine cause it never is.
Smile and you will see me happy for just one moment.
Need is such a strong word, well not really, but it is.
Pictures look back at only the happy memories.
Sweet kisses are ever so tempting aren't they?
Dying in your arms was always what I didn't want to do.
Romantic interludes catch my ears and tell me it's not ok.
Invisible is what love is, only you can sure as hell feel it.
Falling in love with you was the dumbest thing I ever did.
Never-ending hatred is what I feel towards you, not love.
Close your eyes and see if I fall in love with another in a
Matter of seconds not moments and hell never days.
Suffering is what you will do without me, and I'm not
Sorry; not one bit.
Hope is what I sleep on at night, which means you'll go to
Heck, not heaven not hell.

CHECKLIST FOR A MOOD EPISODE

In order to recognize the early warning signs of a new mood episode, have clients complete this verbal or written checklist. These differ from person to person, and are different for mood elevations and depressions. The better they are at spotting their own early warning signs, the faster they can get help. Here's an example.

1. Have you had changes in sleep the past week or two?_____
2. Have your moods been out of synch with what's going on around you?
3. Have you had great amounts of energy without much sleep?
4. Is your self-esteem on a roller coaster? Grandiose to suicidal?
5. Are you taking risks with your sexual life, financial life, and career?
6. Are you unable to concentrate or complete simple tasks?
7. Have you taken on too many projects or duties at work lately?
8. Do you have thoughts of death as an alternative to coping with your stress?
9. Have you changed your appearance significantly the past several weeks? (tattoos, piercings, clothing, haircuts, colorings, etc.)
10. Are you taking your medications as prescribed? Are you using legal or illegal substances with or in place of your medications? Be honest.

Once a person with bipolar I disorder is stabilized with meds, counseling, and perhaps even a mood disorder support group, a recovery process may take place much the same as an alcoholic experiences after being sober for a year. The writing process can then be directed outward to the public, the way any creative and intelligent person would be guided, depending on the "field" or "domain" of the individual. It may be academic, corporate, military, business, or artistic. Many of my clients who have lived lives on the edge have said to me, "I should write a book." To start them on their way, I encourage them to begin with small scenes or "sketches." A sketch is a slice of life scene in which only the bare essentials are filled in, the focus being a glimpse at plot, setting, character, or theme. Dialog is crucial in a sketch, and so I ask those clients who would like to actually write about themselves to do a sketch of something which actually happened in their lives, by doing the following.

SKETCH

Begin writing a "scene" in your life which is important to you. It may contain powerful emotions, so I want you to change the names of your characters from those who were actually there. Once you do that, focus on the conflict between them. Describe them quickly, using the most important physical details only. Remember the lawyer in *Great Expectations* was represented mostly by his five-o'clock shadow! Focus on the time immediately before the climax of the interaction, and the time immediately after. Use dialog, conflict and symbolism, along with any other techniques, and try to stay away from the clichéd ending which involves saying, "It was only a dream."

Another way to write a sketch is to imagine several people in an enclosed space, such as an elevator, hospital room, jail cell, or bus, and put them under some kind of stress or precipitating conflict. Imagine two dogs are fighting in the street and the neighbors come out to break it up. What would they say and do to each other?

A third way is to pretend you are eavesdropping on someone talking on the telephone, or sitting behind a potted plant while two people are having an argument, or write down a conversation you actually overheard in a coffee shop, bus stop, or concert intermission. Sketches are important ways to move material out of journals and poetry, into the realm of fiction because they help writers leave subjectivity and move toward the outer world, to understand the dialog, thoughts and feelings of others dealing with conflicts other than those of the writer.

THE LETTER

Any unfinished business with a family member or caretaker, partner, abuser, or any individual from a client's past can be partially externalized by using a letter format addressed to that person. According to Friedman (1980) Sacks was the first one to document the use of the letter in therapy in 1973. The client is encouraged to write a letter to a parent(s) where issues originate. The client directs the letter away from husband, child, etc. and connects on psychodynamic issues. The other family members or husband can act as coach or double as the letter is read and feelings are expressed. This can empower the clients not only in the session, but also in using the techniques outside of the counseling time.

LETTER TO DAD (OR MOM) IN NEWSPAPER FORM

This exercise should be dictated from the younger client to the therapist who writes the letter in the form of a newspaper, reporting the events of the child's life. Notice how completely you have to get into the child's world to find enough to write about, and how many of Alex's concerns we were able to squeeze into a page of writing to let dad know what Alex is worried about. The therapist or parent needs to remember all of the important aspects of being eight years old. This format also makes writing to seem like a kind of a game rather than a school assignment.

ALEX'S NEWSPAPER HEADLINE:

Alex and Kim went to Seattle. To get there they had to fly two planes. They saw grandma and grandpa and Ashley and Eric. Pam and Bobby were there along with Richard. They did a whole bunch of things: 1) We waited for the airport van to pick us up. 2) Alex and Kim checked their baggage. We got Goldfish, cereal, nuts, and soda. I bought two necklaces, one from the Space Needle, and the other one was in the airport store. We got on a ferry boat and rode to an island that had an old Army boat. It was an hour ride. Everybody went. We saw jellyfish, and Eric saw a dead squid, and Alex saw a live squid when he was on the ferry boat.

ALEX MIGHT VISIT DAD THIS SUMMER!

Things Alex would like to know about dad's house: 1) How many bedrooms? 2) Who's going to be with dad? Anybody besides mom and dad? 3) Snow mobiling? Can we fish and go four-wheeling? Are there any friends Alex's age? 4) Alex would like to teach dad how to play Yahtze. 5) Alex would like some pictures to remember his trip by. Alex remembers taking a bath in the sink at dad's old house in Montana.

ALEX STARTS THIRD GRADE THIS FALL AT LINDER ELEMENTARY SCHOOL

This summer Alex has been at Prime Time. The three best activities were soccer, tetherball, and swimming. His best friends there are Kenny, Chad, Scott. Alex would like to say to Dave, "Don't forget, I'd like to show you how good a soccer player I am. Sincerely yours, Alex. Another handy format to use in the journalistic format involves using the "Who, What, Where, Why, When, and How" format to help clients generate writing about their lives. The client spends the day as the subject of his or her own reporting activity. The format works like this:

(Who)_____

(did What) _____

(Where did they do it?) _____

_____

(Why did they do it?)_____

_____

(When did they do it?)_____

_____

(How did they do it? This one involves specific details of all the activities.)_____

_____

_____

_____

_____

PORTRAIT OF YOUR FATHER/ LETTER TO YOUR FATHER

This exercise comes from my book *The Feeling Process: A Workbook for Men*, and provides a structure for people in therapy who are beginning to deal with their family of origin issues. To begin with you first paint a portrait of your father or male caretaker, including step fathers, boyfriends of your mother who were significant, or other male figures. This asks clients and students to specifically describe fathers or father figures with respect to their characteristics. Then, the letter is written which addresses problem areas in the relationship between clients and that person. Here is a portrait of my own father as an example.

My father, Ray Flick, is an important figure in my life. He nearly qualified for the 1936 Olympics, placing seventh in the Olympic trials in Kansas City. At six feet, three inches and 165 pounds, I still have pictures of him flying over the low hurdles, his golden hair tousled over his forehead, a look of fierce concentration on his face. He attended the University of Kansas on a track scholarship during the Depression, took courses in

Journalism and English, and as he was about to graduate, met my mother.

My dad suffered a toxic relationship with his own father. This anger he carried throughout his life and interfered with his career, his marriage, and his children. Grandpa Flick was a frustrated, non-supportive nomad who saw himself as an entrepreneur. He once owned the recipe for Dad's Cookie Company, which became very successful after he sold it to someone else, and he spent most of his time and energy trying to develop some impossible scheme into financial success. He raised my dad in the repressive atmosphere where children were to be "seen and not heard." He physically and psychologically subjugated him and shamed him so deeply that even in his late adult life, my father wouldn't own more than one or two pairs of shoes, fearing that his internalized Father/Critical Parent would rise up and abuse him for using up family resources!

Without acceptance from his father, Ray Flick, my dad, had a tremendous need for acceptance from people, even strangers, and so he carried this need into his teaching career, his career as a Congregational Minister, his career as a printer, and his role as a husband and father. When he didn't receive this acceptance, it triggered his rage from childhood. My dad had a religious experience as a young man, which I never got him to talk about before he died because I was so resistant to that type of experience. This moment in his life was so formative that he attended Pacific School of Religion to become a minister in the church. When he was a young dad, he was busy in the community as a minister, looking for this acceptance from his congregation. My sister and I both had to work through the resentment of having to share both our parents with needs of the "flock" which he led.

Ray carried the anger towards his father all his life, and he only came to grips with it as he was dying of lung cancer. He knew the anger was there, but he never learned how to let it go; consequently, this anger enveloped him, causing him to be asked to leave his teaching position in Kansas and his last church in California. He then took a job as a printer to help support the family. "I'm the only man I know who went from wearing a black collar to a blue collar," he used to joke. It seemed then that he tried to withdraw from us in total defeat and shame, punishing himself further. He and my mother slept in separate beds; then, he put on over sixty pounds, going from 190 to 250 pounds during his 40s. He began working evenings to avoid interacting with my mother at night.

This portrait, however, partial, contains the seed of the "dynamic" which I share with my father. The word dynamic in psychology means that human acts are understandable through an analysis of the previous experiences and motivational states of the person, rather than through a simple response to the stimuli temporarily preceding the action. The dynamic psychologist (Harry Stack Sullivan) says that we can understand our behavior by looking at our families much more so then we can by looking at isolated traumas (a la Freud), or simple cause-and-effect explanations (B.F. Skinner).

As I write this portrait, I see at least one characteristic that I share with my father, which may clarify the way in which his influence permeated my behavior, for better or for worse. First, I have struggled for acceptance in my teaching career in much the same way dad struggled as a minister. I also carried a lot of anger from this struggle. Eric Berne calls this game "Look How Hard I'm Trying." I had unusual approaches to everything I did, but I had difficulty performing some of the mundane tasks of teaching. I was a brilliant teacher with innovative, stimulating and creative classes which filled up the first fifteen minutes of registration. However, I failed to be competent outside of the classroom with committees, faculty senate, curriculum, and eventually the tenure file itself. The job put me in the old "struggle" to obtain the approval of my colleagues, and this in turn brought up all my anger when they didn't see how hard I was trying in my own way.

Write a portrait of your father or male caretaker or role model, similar to the one above. Write the portrait as a story of his life, a saga or myth in which you use what you remember, what he told you himself and what others in your family told you. It's helpful to talk with others to discover gaps in your knowledge. There are still periods of my father's life that I confuse or have forgotten, and my sister and my Aunt Carrie help me with the facts. Write in any sequence you find important, focusing on what is most important to you. When you are done, see if there are any patterns in his life which are similar to yours.

Break the portrait up roughly like this:

1. Physical description._____
2. Father's childhood._____
3. Father's education._____
4. Father's story of meeting your mother._____
5. Father's career, work, dreams._____
6. Your relationship to your dad._____
7. One "dynamic" or pattern you share with your father._____
8. Things your father taught you._____
9. Rituals you shared with him._____
10. Negative character traits of your father._____
11. How your father affected your ability to be a parent yourself._____
12. Unresolved issues or conflicts in your life that stem from your father._____
13. Where are you with your father currently?_____
14. What can you do to let go of unresolved issues with him?_____

Whatever comes up concerning this portrait, write it down. Don't try to fit it into the format if it doesn't flow. Write what you feel you most need to write at the moment and follow the energy.

LETTER TO YOUR FATHER
Write a letter to your father and tell him how you feel about him right now. Write him about any feelings you are having after doing the portrait. What do you need from him? What did he give you? What was he unable to give you? What would you say to him if he were standing in the room and able to "hear" what you had to say? How does your relationship affect your life now? What would you like to let go of? Write without censoring your responses.

_____
_____
_____
_____
_____
_____
_____

PORTRAIT OF YOUR MOTHER

My mom, Doris Thompson Flick, grew up in the Depression, and her personal background was extremely difficult as well. Doris' mother was a paranoid schizophrenic, and her father had to leave the family to escape the ravages of the mother's disruptive behavior. From the age of two until graduation from high school, my mom was raised by nuns in a residential girl's school in Kansas City. It is a miracle she lived to become a productive member of this society, given what we now know about the nurturing needs of young children. However, having no parents to care for her created an underlying anxiety caused by fear of abandonment and lack of attachment from her earliest years. This anxiety produced a need for control which made it difficult to be her child.

She attended the University of Kansas on a scholarship studying music and English. She won a poetry prize during a university competition, but in her senior year her mother tried to come live with her and make Doris take care of her. She met my father who was graduating that year, and they married and left Kansas to get away from the malevolent influence of Hulda, her birth mother.

Apparently, Doris was pregnant with my sister, and Ray Flick's mother had arranged an abortion for Doris in Stockton, California. However, the young couple changed their minds and kept the baby, my sister Carol. As a young mother Doris wrestled with the demons of her own childhood abandonment, and as I grew up, I learned that to earn my mother's love, I had to listen to her primal "pain." I grew to know women as I knew my mother, as creatures who needed to be taken care of psychologically. Her childhood made it difficult for me to separate from her in my early adult years.

Doris' neurotic needs made me angry and resentful: a child needs someone in the family who understands and feels good about being the nurturing Parent, caring for the actual biological child that he or she is. Instead, I tried to become my mother's Parent, her missing father. This was the biggest stumbling block in my life with women. I ended up picking partners who needed to be taken care of instead of women who could take care of themselves. Also, my mom's background created an adult who grappled with depression. I remember spending a lot of time alone even though I needed her a lot. Many of my childhood struggles and adolescent rebellions were carried out against her since my father seemed to need my love too much to risk setting limits on me.

My mother was also terrified of women who give me something and who were overtly sexual or attractive. I spent much of my dating life and married life looking for the woman who was both nurturing and sexual, and who could give me what was missing from my young life. The women who threatened my mother were the ones for whom she felt I would abandon her.

Doris was an attractive, dark-eyed, intelligent and creative young woman who was attempting to raise two children while she herself had endured a childhood devoid of nurturing. She taught me to talk to and understand women, but she had a hard time letting go of me. For many years I pursued this fantasy of my missing mother in sloe-eyed brunettes, who always needed nurturing until I could feel and let go of the pain of this early relationship.

Write a portrait of your mother, similar to the one of your father.

1. Write a brief physical description_____

_____

2. Describe her childhood_____

_____

3. Write about her education_____

_____

4. Mother's story of meeting your father_____

_____

5. One significant story she told you about her early adult life (18-25) _____

6. Mother's career, work, dreams for her children _____

7. One dynamic pattern you share with your mother, i.e. struggle for acceptance. _____

8. Describe some closeness you had with your mom and routines or rituals you and she shared together. _____

9. Things she taught you. _____

10. Negative aspects of you and your mother's relationship. _____

11. As you write this, describe where you are with your mother now. Use the next pages to complete the portrait. Remember, it's more important to write whatever comes up than to stick to the format of the questions.

LETTER TO YOUR MOTHER

As you did for your father, now write a letter to your mother, telling her how you feel about her now. What qualities within you do you feel are the result of her influence, both positive and negative? If there is something you could do and she could "hear" your request, what would that be? Are there unresolved issues between you at this moment? How are these like the unresolved conflicts with other females in your life now? What would you like to thank her for? Remember, the questions are only to get you started. Write whatever comes up naturally.

_____
_____
_____
_____
_____
_____
_____
_____
_____
_____

FAMILY DYNAMICS

The parents you are writing about are the people they were five, ten, twenty years ago, stuck in the quagmire of their own unmet needs as young people, not the people they are now. This is an important distinction to hold on to as you begin to deal with any childhood experience. For some clients and students, there may be responses based on severe abandonment, physical and sexual abuse, by one or both parents, or by other care takers. Remember, a dynamic means "propelled by previous experiences and motivations of the person learned in the family." For example, my mother was very critical; that was her defense against abandonment. I grew up trying to please her by being good, being a writer, a musician, and a teacher, but I still struggle with the feeling that I'm going to be criticized and rejected, even though I have become excellent in those three areas. When I try to please and they don't notice, I get angry. Eric Berne calls this dynamic (game), "Look How Hard I'm Trying."

I remember D.H. Lawrence's books *Sons and Lovers* and *Women in Love* as influential models for depicting family dynamics in literature. The movie *Out of Africa* is also very useful in helping clients understand how childhood dynamics of Pursuer and Distancer are portrayed in the relationship of Meryl Streep and Robert Redford characters.

Write about your family dynamics, dysfunctional patterns or behavior. For example, do you have to screw up to get attention?

_____
_____
_____
_____
_____
_____

WRITING TO HELP PEOPLE WITH ANXIETY DISORDERS

Anxiety Disorders affect about 40 million adults age 18 years and older in a given year, causing them to be filled with fearfulness and uncertainty, according to the *National Institute of Mental Health* pamphlet on the subject (2007). "Each anxiety disorder has different symptoms, but all the symptoms cluster around excessive, irrational fear and dread (NIMH pamphlet, p. 2, 2007)."

Anxiety Disorders cover a plethora of conditions which are in this list: panic disorder, obsessive-compulsive disorder (OCD), post-traumatic stress disorder (PTSD), social phobia or social anxiety disorder, specific phobias, and generalized anxiety disorder (GAD). These disorders can often be accompanied by other serious problems, such as depression, drug abuse, alcoholism, agoraphobia and others.

In general, anxiety disorders are treated with medication, specific types of psychotherapy, including Cognitive-Behavioral Therapy, or both. "The cognitive part helps people change the thinking patterns that support their fears, and the behavioral part helps people change the way they react to anxiety-provoking situations (NIMH, 2007, p. 9)."

A MARRIAGE GONE WRONG:
ANXIETY FROM PTSD IN DEB'S JOURNAL

One writing exercise which has proven to be extremely effective comes from Donald Michenbaum, PhD's compendium on PTSD called A *Clinical Handbook/ Practical Therapist Manual (for PTSD)*, 1994, pps. 138-142). Here is an example of a former client writing about issues arising from a traumatic experience being in a marriage gone wrong.

I had no idea that the woman who had survived her husband's trying to kill her with poison would be so receptive to this particular exercise from Meichenbaum's book. Deborah's husband I had diagnosed without ever meeting him—Narcissistic Personality Disorder. He liked the fact that she was the one who worked, raised the children and took care of the house; however, he had affairs with many women, professed to be "in real estate" and spent money the family didn't have. Then he met a young girl who attended a local university and decided he wanted to marry her, but his debts and his family were now an inconvenience to his latest fantasy, so he began to put arsenic into his wife's food. (The Scott Peterson Trial is over, and as I write this, it is beginning to sound a lot like Chuck and Scott had much in common.) She worked as a Certified Nurse's Assistant at a convalescent home during this whole experience and almost never missed a day of work. Someone at the assisted living facility got her to see the doctor there who was able to diagnose her symptoms.

Meanwhile, Deb's husband began a campaign to convince local authorities that she was "crazy," by first using her accusations against her. He then called Health and Welfare to accuse her of abuse and neglect. When his young paramour discovered he was married, she left him immediately, and he then asked Deborah if he could come back and work on the marriage! Fortunately, she said no.

During the time of her therapy, Deborah was understandably "shaky" about her reality since it was under assault from the person she was closest and most intimate with. Deb had been an adopted child whose parents were loving, kind and trusting. I think her education was the factor which helped her come to grips with what had happened to her and to plunge herself into this assignment so effectively.

Here are Deb's written answers to the questions in Meichenbaum's book. Deb was a well-educated woman with a Liberal Arts Bachelor's Degree, and she was extremely motivated. A therapist can't expect all of his or her clients to respond the same way. Deb and I used this writing in her therapy, and she read most of it aloud to me as we reviewed the lingering effects of anxiety from her PTSD. Clients can use the bold headings to respond on a separate piece of paper or in their journals.

DIFFICULTY SLEEPING

I used to be a sound sleeper, but now I wake up during the night and have insomnia. I usually sleep well three nights a week, and don't sleep well three nights—give or take a day. Thoughts make it hard to sleep. If I'm not totally exhausted, it takes about two hours to get to sleep. If I awaken, it's usually around four or five a.m. My dreams are disturbing to me, and are similar in content, but different in setting—usually about me trying to get away from wherever I am, or about "Chuck." I hate to wake up and usually feel like it's "another day to get over with." I dread going to bed every night. I dread not being able to sleep or waking up, or what I may dream. I have awakened crying or crying out many times—Chuck would wake me up when I did or I would wake up myself. Mainly I dream about Chuck doing things to me and being scary to me and me trying to get away or figure out what to do.

ATTENTION AND MEMORY

I constantly think about things and sometimes have a hard time pulling myself out of my thoughts. I used to be more attentive, less thoughts about myself. My interests in reading material have changed considerably. I like to read, but don't often. I like the TV on, but don't pay much attention to it – I have to make myself focus on a show that I really want to watch. My mind wanders. I don't really trust anyone, but feel secure in being aware that they may not be trustworthy rather than too trusting like I was before. I remember things in detail, always have. I often switch from subject to subject or scene to scene in my mind. If I'm very upset, I can't concentrate at all.

CURRENT LEVEL OF FUNCTIONING

Things have been better with Child Support, getting the house paid up, no impending doom in sight – but I still feel sad and alone. Better financially, still fighting psychologically. I cry easily and frequently, but I have reason to. More depressed, anxious only if I'm worried about or dreading something. Fears that seem unrealistic to others and that I still have a hard time believing but somehow keep turning out to be real fears. I often feel real upset but know why. Not knowing what might happen to me still, living down and/or with people's views about me, wanting the truth to be told, known, and believed. I would like closure, or at least assimilation, and also a new/different outlook. Loss of loved ones although not through death, was the hardest and I went through a period of "mourning" for each person I had lost. But the worst thing was the loss of my "reality" – everything I had believed was suddenly different. I was more trusting, more naïve before, but now I'm more self-assured and in touch with myself. I like the changes in my personality, but I'm tired of dealing with all this and being sad. I'm more aware of things that might happen in this world. I think most people are sheep. I get along with people because I'm nice and I try to make a point of getting along with people. Besides going to sing karaoke, I don't wish to participate in other activities. I can't relate to people. I don't want to see people I used to know. A good day is just doing normal daily things and not thinking about stuff. A bad day is when I think about it a lot or feel listless. I am quiet and serious on a bad day.

I never planned on being divorced and now having to raise five kids alone. Plus my "history." I have started drinking more often than in the past, but more because of circumstances, such as being single again and friendless, and having to go to a bar to sing. It doesn't help to drink as coping because I don't feel less miserable when I drink and I've had to "cope" to survive. If anything it may help me sleep better. I don't believe that all use is abuse and I have not been prone to abuse in the past, so I don't feel I abuse alcohol and it does not interfere with my every day life. I drink once a week only when my ex has the kids and I'm off work. I feel comfortable talking in therapy, and I also feel comfortable confiding in my boss at work about some things and she helped me – she saved my house.

PAST LEVEL OF FUNCTIONING (PREMORBID ASSESSMENT)

Everything was utopia before. I thought things were good, normal, happy, content, and secure. I thought I was fine. Now I know I was grossly ignorant. I was getting along fine with everyone, except I had some minor issues with a couple people…family was fine. I was fortunate to have God on the side of the truth. I could never have imagined that this could have happened to me.

COPING STRENGTHS

I've coped as well as I could. I haven't coped well, but I went through a lot. I think I've sorted out as much as I can, but I still feel the need to go over it. I want to replace the memories with better ones. I have situations now that I didn't have to deal with before. I don't handle situations well. I kept waking up. My kids, I did it for them.

LINGERING IMPACT

My overall situation is adjusting to life without Chuck in our lives. Recently I have begun to get child support, which has improved my outlook financially. I know that Chuck still has evil intentions towards me. The divorce has changed everything I had planned on for raising my family. Finding out that my husband had been behind all that happened to me went against everything that I previously believed. I'm sure I will never be the same. I have no one but my children. I have made progress, but do not feel "normal."

RUMINATIONS

I have thought about these events constantly for four years and am trying to break away from these memories. I think about what he did to me then, and I understand it now, but then I didn't know what was happening. Now, I would do everything differently, but I realize that at the time, I could only react to it, especially when he got me committed to the psych hospital. I don't blame myself for how I reacted. I blame my husband, but others too, for listening to him and not believing me and for deserting me. Another thing which helped me get out of it was some "happy coincidences" and a snowball effect.

INTRUSIONS

My ex-husband killing me, being arrested, having the kids taken away, losing my house, raising my kids alone. I dream about Chuck a lot. My marriage and my husband weren't what I thought they were. I feel like I always have to be careful. I have had many flashback situations. I have to try very hard to keep my composure. Sometimes I can't. I was afraid of people for a long time, but I am getting better. Everything in my life was affected by what happened, and all of my relationships are still estranged.

AVOIDANCE

I avoid family gatherings, certain people, and cops. I avoid memories of before. I feel like I didn't have control of my life before. I avoid my bedroom, the backyard, most of it happened at home. I cry easily and frequently, but do not feel other emotions as much, just frustration and sadness. I am restrained about people I don't know very well. it's my camouflage. Besides trying not to cry in public, I never showed shame for something I didn't do, I held my head up. I cried for a long time.

PHYSICAL SYMPTOMS

I get startled, but less since Chuck left. I am angry towards Chuck and family members who believed him and cops when I have to deal with them. When someone comes up behind me or opens a door suddenly, I jump. There is a lot of tension in my hands and jaw. I have bouts of shaking or palsy sometimes. Other than not sleeping, I have no real health problems.

If Deb had not lived through this, she might be able to turn this into a classic Stephen King style movie script, but she probably won't. The stress, pain, disillusionment and defensiveness Deb is coping with amounts to a complete change in her world view. I feel that being in a bad marriage is like being wrapped in very dark Saran Wrap and walking around one's life seeing the world through that darkness. It is because we have allowed ourselves to be vulnerable to someone and to trust them, literally with our lives. Deb's experience has changed her completely, and it will affect all of her relationships in the future.

Cognitive Therapy has been clinically proven to be the most effective treatment for disorders in the anxiety group. The therapist says by implication to the client, "If I can change the way you think, I can change the way you feel." One of the processes operating here is simply the therapist using new and positive cognitions or thoughts during the therapy to replace the exaggerated worry and tension they feel, even there is little or nothing in their lives which could have provoked it. It often takes months to get clients to try the thought processes, to find a "mantra" which works for them, and to collect an arsenal of coping tools they will use to fight their anxiety.

Clients can read, write, and verbalize these replacement thoughts during therapy and away from the office. Here are some I have in my journal to fend of anxiety for issues of my own. These are from *Thoughts and Feelings, Second Edition* by McKay, Davis and Fanning. Write your reaction to them as you say them out loud or silently to yourself. These are the actual words you say to yourself as you begin coping with an upcoming stressful situation, such as speaking before the non-fiction writer's group I recently addressed.

1) Preparing
I can handle this, I've done it before.
I can relax rather than get tight.
I'll take one thing at a time.
I'll make a plan for coping
Turn off the worry and do something.

2. Confronting the stressful situation
It will be over soon enough.
No scary thoughts. Stop!
I'll follow each step of my plan.
If I take care of myself, I'll be all right.
I won't worry about what others think.

3. Coping with emotional arousal
Where is my body tight? I can relax it.
Concentrate on breathing.
I'll tighten, then relax my stomach.
Breathe deeply and think only of coping.
Negative thoughts are the enemy. Stop them now.
(My own: The audience doesn't want you to be up tight (musical or lecture).)

4. Reinforcing success
I can turn off my worry now.
I relaxed and made it through.
I'm getting good at coping under stress.
I'm not so afraid of things.
I did a good job just then.

Have you or your clients write about these or talk about them, especially the ones that actually work! The ones that work, work because the client actually uses them! It's as simple as that.

REWRITE YOUR LIFE

Pretend, imagine, revise or change your entire life by doing this exercise. Begin with your birth and imagine a new set of parents, or change the old ones into people whose lives are completely ready to receive you. Creatively rebirth yourself. I'm again following Eric Erickson's stages of development for you to follow as a model.

1. Create a psychologically sound scene into which you are born._____

_____

_____

_____

_____

2. Create a home environment which is perfect for you as an infant and a toddler. Who is taking care of you? Describe your home and the first two years of life. Revise the outcomes of major conflicts which you are aware of that your parents experienced from ages 2-4. Describe the antithesis of any problems, issues, abandonment or dislocation. From your point of view, show the development of your Inner Child during this time in a positive way. Reparent your small self the way you would like to have been raised.

___

3. During the years 5-8, take specific incidents from your childhood and rewrite them. This stage is focused on Initiative versus Guilt. For example, my parents had a fight over my not doing the dishes. Before I know it, my dad is packing his bags and moving out. I told my mother I was sorry, and she said, "It's too late to be sorry." This is my primal scene, and where I learned that if I took on the responsibility and guilt of my parents' relationship, that I would be behaving in a way that my mother wanted me to. I can now rewrite this inserting the personalities of two parents who were not acting out their own conflicts and abandonment issues from their own families of origin. During this time my parents were enacting a psychological game which I have called "I'm Leaving, do you Love Me."

___

4. The period from 7-12 is typically referred to as the "latency" period. Erickson refers to the issues (see page 29) of this period as Industry versus Inferiority. "Between childhood and adulthood, then, our children go to school, and school skill seems to many to be a world all by itself, with its own goals and limitations, its achievements and disappointments" (Erikson, 1968, p. 123). Industry refers to learning to achieve recognition by producing things. "The danger of this period is the development of estrangement from himself and his tasks—the well known sense of inferiority." Nothing that he or she does seems to count with family, school, or peers. Rewrite moments which you can remember, that reflect the feeling that you didn't "count" or matter in your environment. Take specific scenes and change the outcome, so your latent self can focus on receiving recognition for something you produced.

___

5. The period from 12-18 focuses on our identity, literally with what in the world do we choose to identify. In general, it is an inability to settle on a sexual and occupational identity which most disturbs young people says Erikson. The word identify means similar or alike in many ways, to associate in feeling, interest, and action. Make a list of everything you identified with as an adolescent, including teachers, sex objects, athletes, musicians, writers, criminals, rebels, artists, lawyers and others whom you literally wanted to be. In my case it was my high school English teacher, my college sociology teacher, Hemingway, Camus, John Coltrane, Jung and Rollo May, and a host of athletes. Where do your parents fit or not fit on this list? Rewrite crossroads in your life which would have made a difference in your sexual and occupational identities? I rejected my mother's wish for me to be a classical pianist at age nine, but two years later I picked up the saxophone and could play it by ear, and I continue to play to this day. After my mother died and I met Loretta, I bought a synthesizer and began to learn keyboard again, and I continue to the present, seventeen years later!

_____

_____

_____

_____

_____

6. The young person who has not settled the questions of sexual and occupational identity will avoid intimacy or will throw him or herself into promiscuity or serial monogamy. Late in adolescence he or she may settle for highly stereotyped interpersonal relations and come to retain a deep sense of isolation. From 18 to 30 we process the issues of intimacy versus isolation. Rewrite all of your relationships and job experiences to have them turn out the way you now wish them to have turned out
Go over every person you ever fantasized on, slept with, lived with or married. Recreate your entire career and include every job you ever had, including what was going on with you at that time.

_____

_____

_____

_____

_____

In America's 21st century we have two more stages of life beyond the age of thirty, and one of these comes from a book called *The Second Middle Age*. This is primarily because of the life expectancy we enjoy and because of profound changes in the economy. The period from 30 to 40 years old ends up having no name in Erikson's schema. Ultimately, this seems odd because all of the other stages seem to lead up to this one because ultimately we can be evaluated and judged by our successes and failures by this time. F. Scott Fitzgerald said, "There are no second acts in American life," meaning that if the first act doesn't grab you, don't wait around for what comes next. After the first act, everything is downhill, including the realities of adult life which replace the adolescent dreams. The thirties are some of the most productive years we have for several reasons. Marriage, child raising, occupational competence, social mobility, material success, travel, and additional education occur because people at this age have energy, experience, and competence to propel them through the "Multi-tasking" years. Working adults on average change their careers, jobs, or avocations once every ten years. Middle-age is statistically around 35-36 years because men die at age 72. Women live approximately six years longer than men. But we are in better health now than we were fifty years ago, and are not ready to be "thrown away" in our corporate jobs at age 55 when we are supposedly less productive! There is a second middle age, beginning around 55 during which we have to reinvent ourselves.

Robert Bly writes that if one has been plugged into the corporate structure for the early years, he or she must move into a self-directed phase after the corporation has down-sized one. If the reverse is true, if one has spent the earlier years raising children, focusing on a family and supporting a breadwinner, that individual has to move into the outer world to complete his or her growth and development.

7. The Multitasking stage is the most stressful stage of development for Americans. Make a list of events which have taken place in your life from 30-40 and measure it against the Holmes Stress Scale which follows. From 30 to 40 these events happened to me. 1) Obtained Master's Degree 2) Was divorced and separated from my twins 3) Left the first love of my life 4) Moved 5) Worked in a lumber mill 6) Tried to get a teaching job 7) Married my second wife 8) Moved to Hawaii 9) Got a tenure-track teaching job 10) My son Jacob was born 11) My father died and mom had emphysema 12) Separated and eventually divorced my second wife 13) Worked as a psych counselor and English instructor for two years 14) My mother passed away 15) I finally resolved my Intimacy versus Isolation issues 16) Met and married my wife of 23 years. 17) Was denied tenure at the community college where I worked 18) Moved to San Diego. I'll never forget a goal workshop I was doing at the psych unit where I worked in Hawaii. After six months I looked at my list of goals and it finally dawned on me that no normal human being could accomplish the things I had on my list. That's when I began to suspect that I had Adult Attention Deficit Disorder. My list was simply not "doable."

Now, create your list of issues or transitions you have undergone during your "Multi-tasking" stage of your life.

_____
_____
_____
_____
_____

8. Erikson's stage of development from 40 plus onward is called Generativity versus Stagnation. The former is primarily the concern for establishing and guiding the next generation. The latter is indicated by regression to an obsessive need for pseudo intimacy which takes place with a pervading sense of stagnation, boredom, and interpersonal impoverishment. Individuals begin to "indulge" themselves as if they were their own only child. What might be helpful here for the clients is for them to imagine or visualize themselves in the final three stages if they are not that old, and project what their lives will be like if they continue to live, feel and function the way they are now. For example, can you see yourself with your husband (or wife) in ten or twenty years together when the children are gone? Will you travel together, join the Peace Corps, adopt Greyhounds, volunteer? Continue learning? Or will you stagnate as soon as the children leave and there's an "empty nest?" Imagine the time when you and your partner return from the graduation of your youngest child and you enter the house you've lived and write about what exciting plans you have together or describe the stagnation you expect to encounter when the two of you have to reacquaint?

_____
_____
_____
_____
_____
_____
_____
_____

9. Integrity versus Despair involves the client and the therapist in an interesting dilemma. A positive view of aging or seniority, involves having some contact with an older person that has been positive. If the client sees the aging person as someone who has "taken care of things and people, and has adapted himself to the triumphs and disappointments of being, the originator of others and the generator of things and ideas—only in him the fruit of the nine stages gradually ripens. This is integrity.

Loss of this ego integration is signified by disgust and by despair. Despair expressed the feeling that time is short, too short for the attempt to start another life. The individual has contempt for himself and his choices, that death is not a finite boundary to life. Eric Berne has great name for this game which is "Waiting for the Undertaker."

The individual hides behind misanthropy, displeasure, of institutions and particular people. This is the loser's script at the final curtain. This is where some people who have lived a totally circumscribed life try to buy their way into heaven when they find a preacher or a church which really tweaks their guilt and they sell their family home and give the money to a group. Think of Jim Jones and his flock in Guyana and how the people felt at the end of their lives after handing them over to a madman who enslaved them? By writing about the older people in your life, reflect on how and why you feel the way you do about aging and death? And now we're back to the beginning of the book.

_____

_____

_____

_____

_____

WRITING FOR PEOPLE WITH PTSD

Schiraldi writes in *The PTSD Sourcebook*, 2000, "Post-traumatic stress disorder results from exposure to an overwhelmingly stressful event or events, such as war, rape, abuse, airplane crashes, and it is a normal response by normal people to an abnormal situation." The key symptoms for folks with PTSD include recurrent and intrusive recollections of the event (memories), distressing dreams, flashbacks, "triggers," physiological reactivity to cues that symbolize or resemble the traumatic event (*DSM-IV-TR*, 2000).

People with PTSD commonly feel detached or estranged from others and often assume that they are now different and that no one could possibly relate to their experiences (Schiraldi, p. 3). This is where writing can be a tool to share these experiences with the therapist, with a group, or with the wider public. The therapist or group leader needs to know whether or not writing helps the individual move beyond the trauma, or whether it acts as a trigger to flashbacks and re-experiencing the memories in an intrusive way. There are three basic stages in the recovery from PTSD: Victim, survivor, and thriver. When the client is in a victim stage, the only writing which will help is that which is done to identify symptoms. The following exercise is for people in the latter two stages.

Creative Writing for Counselors and Their Clients - Steve Flick M.F.A., LCSW

1. Create and write about a safe space. This has become one of the cliché's of late night television, but creative visualization (Shakti Gawain) is one of the Cognitive Behavioral Therapy's most successful outreach into eastern philosophy. Write about walking to that safe space, including sight, hearing, smell, touch, and taste. Write about all of the feelings which go with creating the safe space.

_____

_____

_____

_____

2. Create a volume knob, a light switch, a toggle switch, or a breaker box and imagine that's it's on your chest. Use the switch to identify when triggers, flashbacks or memories are intruding into your day. Describe the memory, then decide whether or not you wish to continue processing the thoughts or if you want to turn them off. Either way, you have control! "I am deciding to continue remembering, or I am deciding to stop."

_____

_____

_____

_____

3. Write a letter to the traumatic incident. Describe the person you are now that you have had the experience. Write about the person you were before, and the person you are now. Write about where you want to be in two or three years. Save, tear up or burn the letter or give it to the therapist or mentor or friend.

_____

_____

_____

_____

PRACTICING WITH FEELINGS

Feeling words tend to be shorter, honest, truthful, and without much intellectualizing. However, one-word answers don't help the therapist see an example of why the clients feel the way they do. So, the sentence can be developed by adding "because" to the writing. For example, "I want to change my hair because the grey makes me feel old some days when I look in the mirror.'

Right now I feel_____

I love_____

I hate_____

I want_____

I need_____

I am changing_____

I am hanging on to_____

Women are_____

Men are_____

Gay people are_____

Bisexuals are_____

Trans-gendered people are_____

My dad is (was)_____

My mom is (was)_____

Death is_____

Children are_____

My living space is_____

I would like to travel to_____

I would like to study_____

My jobs (chores) have been_____

My friends are_____

My love object (partner, significant other, boyfriend/girlfriend) is_____

My future is_____

I'm stuck in_____

I want to change_____

My sibling(s) are_____

My car (bike) is_____

My money (finances) is_____

Every day I feel_____

Creative Writing for Counselors and Their Clients - Steve Flick M.F.A., LCSW

Every day I think_____

Life is_____

My past is_____

Marriage is_____

Living together is_____

Dating is_____

The Internet makes_____

Birth control is_____

AIDS makes me feel_____

I feel my education_____

I can compromise on_____

I can't compromise on_____

Which parent loved you the most?_____

Which parent loved you the least?_____

People can (can't) tell me what they feel_____

I can talk to_____

I can't talk to_____

I need to talk about_____

When I look in the mirror I feel_____

My best physical feature is_____

My worst is_____

My best personality trait is_____

My worst is_____

Commitment is_____

When things get tough, I_____

Christmas is_____

I regret_____

My greatest fear_____

When I was younger_____

When I go to sleep_____

I can_____

The future_____

I wish_____

Creative Writing for Counselors and Their Clients - Steve Flick M.F.A., LCSW

Secretly_____

Time_____

Filling in these blanks makes me_____

Right now I feel_____

POSITIVE, NEUTRAL OR NEGATIVE:
Analyze your responses by marking a "+" for a positive outlook, "o" for a neutral outlook, and a "-" for a negative outlook. There are 45 items in areas of relationships, material world, inner feelings. Just see if your client is struggling with negativity and see where it comes from. Also, this exercise may have captured some inner dialog on the issues brought out by the word combinations. What part of the way you feel now would you like to change?

_____

_____

_____

_____

_____

_____

_____

_____

For me the diagnosis of Posttraumatic Stress Disorder is the description of origin for many of the conditions we see. It's really the Meta-diagnosis from Freudian times to the present. It must be noted that Freud based some of his theories on the Greek drama of Sophocles (525-456 b.c.) formulating the Oedipus Complex and the Electra Complex as well.

Gestalt Psychology utilized Psychodrama which was originated by J.L. Moreno in 1959 and was used by many group therapists (Samuel and Ellen Wood, 1996). If you entered group therapy based on this approach, you would act out your problems or relationship with the assistance and participation of other group members. Sometimes you would play the part of the person who is a problem in your life, a technique called role reversal. You might take the role of your parent, boyfriend, girlfriend, or spouse, and in this way gain some understand of the other person's feelings. "When group members act out their own frustrations and role-play the frustrations of others, they gain insight into their problems and troubling relationships (P. 554, Wood, 1996).

A derivative technique used in individual therapy was called "the empty chair," in which the client explored his or her issues with important individuals by first playing the part of the other, and then by imagining the other sitting in the empty chair and practicing or "rehearsing" the troubling situation with the other party.

WRITING DRAMATIC SCENES OR DIALOGS FOR THERAPY

Drama itself can be used to study family dynamics, and that can be drama from stage, screen, radio, or television. My favorites among many include *Everyday People, Death of a Salesman, Cuckoo's Nest, I never Promised You a Rose Garden, August* by Judith Rossner, and all of O'Neill's plays, which are based on his own dysfunctional family.

I have used a technique frequently in therapy where I play the role of someone with whom my client has issues. It's called a "rehearsal." In it, the client verbalizes his or her feelings to the person over and over until it comes out appropriately using "I" statements. People who are extremely shy or who have anger issues have to rephrase their feelings many times before they can express themselves in person. Writing is extremely helpful in this practice because they can rehearse the dialogs in their journal before they express themselves in person.

TO BE OR NOT TO BE

The issue of suicide, i.e. ideation, vocalization, forming a plan, and a suicide attempt, is a process which is handled by professionals in various ways. As mentioned before, folks with Bipolar I Disorder experience some of the most severe depressions of all, and it's unclear what the best approach is. Many professionals simply call the police (in Idaho) and they come to do any assessment in the office, or else, since the client is safe for the moment, they ask the therapist or PSR worker to transport that person to the nearest emergency room for the evaluation. If the client admits to the suicidal utterance in the presence of the police or the crisis team, he or she may be admitted to the psychiatric facility with an in-patient, locked unit at that time.

Then there is Para-suicide. There are some clients, especially those with Borderline Personality Disorder, who view the hospital as a safe, comfortable, and womblike retreat, where they are surrounded with kind and trained "mommies" and "daddies" to take care of them, provide meals, clean, entertain them with group, art therapy, videos, and yes, a ready-made social life. To them it is like a college dormitory.

There are others, especially in the early years of their treatment, when threatening suicide is an attention-getting behavior which is partially carried out, so that the issues of whether or not they're "really" suicidal is moot, and the mental health system has no choice but to admit them to the hospital. When they actually kill themselves, it's because they sliced their wrists lengthwise instead of across, they took more pills than they realized, or the combination of medications, alcohol and illegal drugs interacted in a lethal way.

The suicide response can be in three stages. The first stage is to have the person talk or write out anything they want to say without interference or direction. I remember vividly, speaking to a woman in the late stages of her cancer asking me if I wouldn't kill myself if I were in her shoes, fraught with pain, taking powerful medications, enduring chemotherapy and radiation, watching her quality of life deteriorate. She told me that she was sitting in her house with a loaded pistol, trying to make up her mind.

I told her honestly that I was studying *Death with Dignity* a process developed by Derek Humphries, the originator of the Hemlock Society. In Idaho we live next to the only state in the U.S. which has legal physician-assisted suicide. I asked if she had thought of that, and she said she hadn't realized that. I told her that's would I would do if in her shoes. It was obvious that she wouldn't have put up with any bullshit answer at that point, so I decided to be honest with her.

This led me to the second stage: Help the person find some reason to live or to not kill themselves for another day. The woman and I searched for something, I told her it didn't matter how miniscule the meaning was. We had already exhausted God and religion, the family, finding a cure, the family pets, others finding her in a pool of blood, a soap opera, doing her living will. It ended up she realized she was not prepared enough to kill herself and would leave too big a mess behind, literally and figuratively, to leave this earth just yet. She also was thinking about sunrises, and knowing she wouldn't be sleeping much that night, she was going to wait for one more.

Since I didn't have her phone number (she had *69ed the crisis line), I asked her for the third stage: Make a contract with me to promise not to kill herself, to get help or call a family member the next day, and to write a list of things she had to complete, before she could allow herself to suicide. She hung up without ceremony after she grudgingly agreed to the contract. "I'm only saying yes because you asked me to," she said. "Tomorrow's another day."

My private feeling is that if I could really talk about suicide and death in a realistic way, it would prevent manipulative clients from abusing the mental health system in the way they do now. My viewpoint is a radical one. What we don't want is a para-suicidal person acting out the drama of suicide and doing a poor job of it. During the course of a self-euthanasia, Humphries recommends a combination of Seconal, Potassium Chloride, and a plastic bag over the head to assure the person he or she would not wake up with severe brain damage or paralysis. The amounts and procedures are outlined in his book. I want total control of when my life is over, assuming I am ill and not in an automobile accident. I believe if we have debilitating, terminal, and degenerative conditions, we have the right to die with dignity. I want to have people around me at the end who agree with me and will let me do it my way. I don't believe there is a 10,000 foot tall god figure waiting to hurl me into heaven or hell. I believe we live in a Puritanical culture which wants to dictate to us how we should treat our bodies at the beginning, middle and end of life.

To that end I have developed the next section to help counselors, teachers, and clients to come to grips with these issues, talk about them, share their feelings with their families, and make sure all health providers comply with those wishes.

On the next several pages, begin your own Living Will for Health Care and Power of Attorney; then, write your obituary and complete the Life Review. Share it with someone close to you, and ask him or her about his wishes for how he wants to deal with the end of his life. Tell stories about people you've known who have passed away, and what you learned from them. With those emotions brought forth, then compose a "Mission Statement" for your life. That format follows.

Here is my experience with the deaths of important people around me. It is a radical (root) approach because currently in this society, the conservative and reactionary elements do not want individuals to have controls over their decisions to give birth or to die. Consequently, one has to have wishes firmly in place in legal documents to prevent a family member from interfering with your death and dying processes. As I write this, Elizabeth Kubler-Ross has passed away at 76. She is the author of one of the most influential books ever written on death and dying and the originator of the hospice movement in this country. *On Death and Dying* is required reading for any therapist grappling with the issues of terminal disease endured by his or her clients.

My mother died completely in control. After ten years of suffering with emphysema, she called me, my sister, and her grand daughters together for a dinner. She asked me to call the nurses at the local hospital anonymously and ask how many Dilaudid it would take to end her life, and they said three. The medication was ground up and put it in her food. She went back to bed, said goodbye to each one of us, and died quietly and painlessly. Once again, in control. Toward the end she was processing some guilt about me and my two divorces, and she said she should have divorced our father instead of hanging on, but I told her to let it go, and that I was all right.

The techniques of the Life Review, Obit, and Living Will all could roughly be called Paradoxical Intentions because instead of reaching for the warm fuzzies, the therapist is reaching for the "short hairs." It usually takes confronting some kind of pain first before a client will let go of his or her defenses. The Paradoxical Intent is the act of prescribing the symptom, just to see what will happen. If the children are fighting too much, ask them to fight more next week than they did this week. There is no research to show why this works, it just seems to in some cases. In this case of paradoxical intention the therapist asks the client to imagine the end of life first to overcome some defenses by feeling the effects of mortality (McKay, Davis, Fanning, p. 179).

This exercise is based on a universal desire in each of us to see how the people around us would feel if we weren't there anymore. The impulse is described in the archetypal scene in Tom Sawyer where Tom and *Huckleberry Finn* attend their own funerals in the church in town. It's based around the feeling that if we're missed enough, perhaps people will treat us differently if we could magically reappear. We could live more fully if someone would only tell us how important we are to him or her. It also reminds me of the scene in the movie *It's a Wonderful Life* where James Stewart observes how the world has not progressed as well without his existence in it. The angel gives him this privileged look at a world minus his unique, individual life.

Another assignment in this group is to have a client read the obituaries in the local paper every day, focusing on what was written about each person, and noticing especially people who die who are close to the same age as one's client. My informal results to this analysis, by the way, show that between 20 and 25 percent of obituaries reveal that the age of death is under sixty.

The most radical activity for the subject of death is the Suicide Note. However, the ego of the client must be highly defended or intellectualized, and the individual should have romanticized suicide as have some rock stars, poets, or movie stars or hold an Existential view of life. Was it Dorothy Parker or James Dean who said, "Life hard, die fast, and have a good-looking corpse?" I personally prefer Lillian Hellman's advice that "The best revenge is living well." And nobody, not even the most hardened, defended neurotic will want to end up like Ivan Illyich in Tolstoy's short story who, while lying in his deathbed, realized he had lived his life all wrong.

A & E also has an excellent video concerning the funeral business in America. It's called *The Business of Death* and was produced in 1999 by A & E television's "Investigative Reports." Have clients watch the video. There is no real or rational reason why we cannot discuss death and dying in a normal conversation without being considered morbid, overly dramatic, or manipulative. For a while I considered working in the funeral industry making long trips with the bodies of the deceased, delivering them to relatives and funerals in other states. The young interns in the funeral business get up in the middle of the night, dress in formal clothing, and remove bodies from their homes and assist grieving families at the moment of losing a loved one. Highly defended clients begin to access some deep fears when they observe the process our culture uses to deal with death.

Children are more likely to encounter death when it happens to a pet in the home. One of my favorite dogs, Buck, was shoved into a well by some sadistic peers in my home town, and my father kept the situation away from me for years until he finally told me at graduation. The way we talk about death to children is very confusing. We say we "lost" Aunt Harriet, or Uncle Joe "passed away" in the night, or Bob was "taken from us to his heavenly rest" while cousin Beth "went to meet her maker." To a literal mind, then, it sounds as if these folks need a search and rescue team and will be returning with frostbite and dehydration!

Gary Landreth, Ph.D., told a story during a seminar of a seven-year-old boy who thought his grandfather was residing in a basement crypt and could be visited and talked to through a ventilation pipe in the cemetery grounds. At any rate, everyone has issues and feelings about death, which are normal and in *Creative Writing for Counselors*, this would be one way to get a dialog started with clients.

Redux: There are eight exercises to help clients focus on mortality: 1) Life Review. 2) Living Will. 3) Swapping stories, narratives of those we know about who've died. 4) Reading obituaries 5) Writing an obituary 6) Suicide Note. 7) Read about the "White Light" stories of people who've died and been resuscitated. 8) Read some literature, fiction or non-fiction, regarding the issue of death, beginning with the works already mentioned. Currently, I am looking at *Final Exit* by Derek Humphries, which deals with the practicalities of self-deliverance and assisted suicide for the dying. 9) Finally, the client writes a Mission Statement, which is a current buzz-word in the corporate world that can help a client articulate what his or her "mission" in life is. That can also include the role of counseling and therapy and give the therapist some guidance as to how that patient views therapy and what he or she expects from it. This reframes the problem at the end of the eight exercises, so that clients can see that all of life is time limited, and priorities for living well have to be set to achieve a full life.

THE EXERCISES: Life Review

I am dying soon, and before I die I wish to make a final statement. It is the truth as I have understood it about who I am, what I believe, how I have really felt. It is my attempt to complete matters before I die.

Name:_____

Date:_____

The people I would like to say goodbye to are these:_____

_____

_____

_____

_____

If I could live my life over again:_____

_____

_____

_____

_____

I would spend more time:_____

_____

_____

_____

_____

I would spend less time:_____

_____

_____

_____

_____

The things I would like to do before I die are:_____

_____

_____

_____

_____

Creative Writing for Counselors and Their Clients - Steve Flick M.F.A., LCSW

The behaviors and attitudes and feelings that held me back and kept me from getting what I wanted are:
_____
_____
_____

The behaviors and attitudes and feelings that I admired in myself and others are:_____
_____
_____
_____

The accomplishments I feel good about are:_____
_____
_____
_____

The people that have had the greatest positive effect on my life are:_____
_____
_____
_____

The thing that is most important to me this day before I die is:_____
_____
_____
_____

Something I've never said to someone that I want to say now:_____
_____
_____
_____

Please put this on my memorial or gravestone:_____
_____
_____
_____

LIVING WILL
A Directive to Withhold or to Provide Treatment

To my family, relatives, friends, physicians, employers, and all others whom it may concern:

Directive made this_____day of_____20_____

I _____(name)

Being of sound mind, willfully and voluntarily make known my desire that my life shall not be prolonged artificially under the circumstances set forth below, do hereby declare:

If at any time I should have an incurable injury, disease, illness or condition certified to be terminal by two medical doctors who have examined me, and where the application of life-sustaining procedures are utilized, or I have been diagnosed as being in a persistent vegetative state, I direct that the following marked expression of my intent be followed and that I be permitted to die naturally, and that I receive any medical treatment or care that may be required to keep me free of pain or distress.

Check One

_____If at any time I should become unable to communicate my instructions, then I direct that all medical treatment, care, and nutrition and hydration necessary to restore my health, sustain my life, and to abolish or alleviate pain or distress be provided to me. Nutrition and hydration shall not be withheld or withdrawn from me if I would die from malnutrition or dehydration rather than from my injury, disease, illness or condition.

_____If at any time I should become unable to communicate my instructions and where the application of artificial life-sustaining procedures shall serve only to prolong artificially the moment of my death, I direct such procedures be withheld or withdrawn except for the administration or nutrition and hydration.

_____If at any time I should become unable to communicate my instructions and where the application of artificial life-sustaining procedures shall serve only to prolong artificially the moment of death, I direct such procedures be withheld or withdrawn including withdrawal of the administration of nutrition and hydration.

In the absence of my ability to give directions regarding the use of life-sustaining procedures, I hereby appoint_____(name) currently residing at _____, as my attorney-in-proxy for the making of decisions relating to my health care in my place; and it is my intention that this appointment shall be honored by him/her, by my family, relatives, friends, physicians and lawyer as the final expression of my legal right to refuse medical or surgical treatment; and I accept the consequences of such a decision. I have duly executed a Durable Power of Attorney for health care decisions on this date.

In the absence of my ability to give further directions regarding my treatment, including life-sustaining procedures, it is my intention that this directive shall be honored by my family and physicians as the final expression of my legal right to refuse of accept medical and surgical treatment, and I accept the consequences of such refusal.

If I have been diagnosed as pregnant and that diagnosis is known to any interested person, this directive shall have full force during the course of my pregnancy.

I understand the full importance of this directive and am emotionally and mentally competent to make this directive. No participant in the making of this directive or in its being carried into effect, whether it be a medical doctor, my spouse, a relative, friend or any other person shall be held responsible in any way, legally, professionally or socially, for complying with my directions.

Signed_____ Date_____

City, County and State of residence_____

The declarant has been known to me personally, I believe him/her to be of sound mind.

Witness_____Witness _____
Address _____ Address _____

A DURABLE POWER OF ATTORNEY FOR HEALTH CARE

DESIGNATION OF HEALTH CARE AGENT

I, _____
　(Insert your name and address)
do hereby designate and appoint _____
　(Insert name, address, and telephone number of one individual only as your agent to make health care decisions for you.) None of the following may be designated as your agent: 1) your treating health care provider, 2) a non-relative employee of your treating health care provider, 3) an operator of a community care facility, or 4) a non-relative employee of an operator of a community care facility), as my attorney in fact (agent) to make health care decisions for me as authorized in this document. For the purposes of this document, "Health Care Decision" means consent, refusal of consent, or withdrawal of consent to any care, treatment, service, or procedure to maintain, diagnose, or treat an individual's physical condition.

CREATION OF DURABLE POWER OF ATTORNEY FOR HEALTH CARE.
　By this document I intend to create a durable power of attorney for health care. This power of attorney shall not be affected by my subsequent incapacity.

GENERAL STATEMENT OF AUTHORITY GRANTED.
　Subject to any limitations in this document, I hereby grant to my agent full power and authority to make health care decisions for me to the same extent that I could make such decisions for myself if I had the capacity to do so. In exercising this authority, my agent shall make health care decisions that are consistent with my desires as stated in this document or otherwise made known to my agent, including, but not limited to, my desires concerning obtaining or refusing or withdrawing life-prolonging care, treatment, services, and procedures. (If you want to limit the authority of your agent to make health-care decisions for you, you can state the limitations in Paragraph 4 ("Statement of Desires, Special Provisions, and Limitations") below. You can indicate your desires by including a statement of your desires in the same paragraph).

STATEMENT OF DESIRES, SPECIAL PROVISIONS AND LIMITATIONS.
　(Your agent must make health care decisions that are consistent with your known desires. You can, but are not required to, state your desires in the space provided below. You should consider whether you want to include a statement of your desires concerning life-prolonging care, treatment, services, and procedures. You can also include a statement of your desires concerning other matters relating to your health care. You can also make your desires known to your agent by discussing your desires with your agent or by some other means. If there are any types of treatment that you do not want to be used, you should state them in the space below. If you want to limit in any other way the authority given your agent by this document, you should state the limits in the space below. If you do not state any limitations your agent will have broad powers to make health care decisions for you, except to the extent that there are limits provided by law.) In exercising the authority under this durable power of attorney for health care, my agent shall act consistently with my desires as stated below and is subject to the special provisions and limitations stated in the living. Herein are contained my additional statement of desires, special provisions, and limitations: (You may attach additional pages if you need more space to complete your statement. If you attach additional pages, you must date and sign each of the additional pages at the same time you date and sign this document.)

_____

_____

DURABLE POWER OF ATTORNEY

This Power of Attorney will not be valid unless it is signed by two qualified witnesses who are present when you sign or acknowledge your signature. If you have attached any additional pages to this form, you must date and sign each of the additional pages at the same time you date and sign this Power of Attorney.)

STATEMENT OF WITNESS
(This document must be witnessed by two qualified adult witnesses. None of the following may be used as a witness: 1) A person you designate as your agent or alternate agent, 2) a health care provider, 3) an employee of a health care provider, 4) the operator of a community care facility, 5) an employee of an operator of a community care facility. At least one of the witnesses must make the additional declaration set out following the place where the witnesses sign.)

I declare under penalty of perjury under the laws of Idaho that the person who signed or acknowledged this document is personally known to me (or proved to me on the basis of convincing evidence) to be the principal, that the principal signed or acknowledged this durable power of attorney in my presence, that the principal appears to be of sound mind and under no duress, fraud, or undue influence, that I am not the person appointed as attorney in fact by this document, and that I am not a health care provider, an employee of a health care provider, the operator of a community care facility, nor an employee of an operator of a community care facility.

Signature:_____

(Print Name)_____
(Residence Address)_____
(Date)_____

(At least one of the above witnesses must also sign)_____

I further declare under penalty of perjury under the laws of Idaho that I am not related to the principal by blood, marriage, or adoption, and, to the best of my knowledge, I am not entitled to any part of the estate of the principal upon the death of the principal under a will now existing or by operation of law.

(Signature)_____(Signature)_____

(Signer of instrument may either have it witnessed as above or have his/her signature notarized as below, to legalize this instrument.)
State of Idaho, County of_____. On this _____day of 20_____ before me personally appeared_____
_____. (full name of signer of instrument.)

to me known (or proved to me on basis of satisfactory evidence) to be the person whose name is subscribed to this instrument and acknowledged that he/she executed it. I declare under penalty of perjury that the person whose name is subscribed to this instrument appears to be of sound mind and under no duress, fraud or undue influence.

_____
(Signature of Notary)

WRITING A MISSION STATEMENT

The point of the previous chapter is to accrue a sense of urgency regarding what it is you'd like to accomplish at your stage of life. A mission statement is a raison d'être or reason for being. It's an answer to the question, "Why am I here? What's my unique purpose in life? This is not as simple as it seems. Many of us had to put aside important goals and other aspects of our lives in order to be married, raise a family, guide or participate in a corporation, educate others, for religious reasons, or to simply survive. This mission statement may require reviving some dreams that have been suppressed or put aside, such as writing a book, painting, playing music, performing in a play, acting, traveling, or altruism, such as joining the Peace Corps. Robert Bly offered this observation, namely that people who have spent their early lives in corporate activity need to leave that world and do something wholly for themselves at the middle of their lives. By the same token, those who have spent the first half of their lives in self-focus need to participate in the larger community.

The reality is one cannot spend his or her entire life at the service of others. The mission statement is an initial step towards reacquainting oneself with one's passion in life. Here are some aspects of a mission statement you could respond to.

What makes (made) me unique as an individual? _____
_____
_____

What did I do earlier in my life that remains unfulfilled in my dream life? _____
_____
_____

What individuals came into my life that helped me be in touch with my reason for being alive?
_____
_____

What do I have a passion for? Where is the energy in my thoughts, dreams, fantasies, reveries, etc.?
_____
_____

Whom do I secretly admire right now? Whom did I emulate in the past? _____
_____
_____

Can I live a new lifestyle that might go along with being a jeweler, writer, painter, Peace Corps volunteer, or world traveler?
_____

What do I see myself doing with some new training or education?
_____

Interview someone who is doing what you want to do. _____
_____
_____

What's the most creative thing you've ever done in your life? _____
_____
_____

Have you ever had an entrepreneurial impulse or idea? _____
_____
_____

Now, take your answers and call someone with whom you can discuss the realities of what you've written. Take a tape recorder with you and tape the interview. Listen to your voice and transcribe the interview. Look for the energy in your voice and interaction with the other person.

I have been thinking about mission statements and forming examples, which might be meaningful for people in therapy. While driving to a small clinic about an hour from my house, I was imagining a wide range of responses to writing a mission statement. You could respond to these if you are having trouble forming your own.

I am here to do God's will. To that end I want to study the Bible, hang out with other religious people of like mind, figure out what that might be, and practice that to the best of my ability. (Develop the implications of this lifestyle.)

I am here to create the best art, music, and writing possible to share my vision of the world. To do that, I have to adopt a certain lifestyle with goals that are different from childrearing, earning a living, or serving others, except through my art (Develop).

I am here to uphold justice, serve, and protect. To that end I will train to be in law enforcement or the criminal justice system (Develop).

I am here to heal the sick, wounded, and the infirm. My life energy will be focused around learning everything I can about the human body (Develop).

I am here to create a family, provide for the family, raise and nurture my children, and inculcate them with my values (Develop).

You can see that each person's mission statement will vary wildly. Some may simply be alive to have as much fun and stimulation as possible before they die. The purpose of this is to make overt the values which motivate you and propel you forward, the values which make you want to get up each day.

Author's Example: My mission statement is to overcome the effect of my early life on myself and to teach others to do the same. I'm here to love, support, and enjoy my relationship with my wife, a relationship that I have helped to create. My passions are music, writing, teaching and counseling. I've been able to do all of them with varying degrees of success. I'm here to experience humility every day I do therapy and counseling with other people, helping them recover atrophied parts of their lives. I'm here to be as healthy as I am at 61, so that I can help other people with their issues. I'm here to heal the relationships with my sons Sim, Nat, and Jake whose mothers and I were unable to stay together.

How I want to die: Additions to my Living Will

I thought I should include my own statement of additional desires, special provisions, and limitations here as an example of some important issues that may come up during the end of life. This living will and durable power of attorney are legal in the state of Idaho. However, if my wife Loretta runs into any problems with my choices regarding how I want to end my life, we can go to Oregon where physician-assisted suicide is legal. We'll rent a motel, see two physicians, say goodbye, and I want to be cremated, half my ashes spread in the Boise River on the Capitol Street Bridge, and half kept by my wife until she can spread the remaining half when she's ready.

After a lifetime of examining the religious ideas of the world, I hold that the Bible and other religious texts are evidence of man's highest aspirations and beautiful metaphors of our spiritual desires. But I do not believe there is a 10,000-foot God who puts us down a laundry chute to hell or opens the gate of heaven according to how we believed. I know in my heart that it's all here on earth, and that heaven and hell are metaphors for how we should live now, and the fact is that "now" is our eternity.

I want complete control over the amount and extent of physical pain and discomfort that I will tolerate. To that end, I want Oxycontin, Dilaudid, Potassium Chloride and Seconal available for me to take if I so choose. Potassium Chloride will stop the heart in less than two minutes, according to Derek Humphries in *Final Exit*, and I hope to have all those medicines available when it's my time to die (Humphries, p. 42). I have made my peace with all of the traditional religious attitudes and values, which may be counter to my beliefs now. Therefore, there will be no priests, ministers or officials of any church at my memorial unless they are my friends or acquaintances. My education, values, and the work I have done on myself and with others has led me to these beliefs.

Completion of these exercises is meant to bring forth dialog of anyone in therapy with his or her family, so that there can't be any legal challenges when you die. We have seen how stressful it is when someone passes away and the relatives disagree on the living will or health care decisions. Ted Williams' nephew froze his body and severed his head and placed him in a cryogenic mausoleum as a result of a lawsuit he filed, contradicting Ted's final wishes. This is some bizarre attempt to explore a belief that Mr. Williams can be revived in the future when the technology is more advanced.

Anyone in your family with reactionary religious values is going to want to challenge some of the provisions, so make sure you follow all of the instructions. Now we come to the Obituary exercise. Write your obituary in the third person, including accomplishments and regrets. You may use the following format, or invent your own. Please spend several days reading obituaries in your local newspaper to see how the family of the deceased communicates the life history of the family member who died.

Birth date, place, time, circumstances._____
_____

2. Schooling and any moves your family made during your youth._____
_____
_____

Major life events, graduations, jobs, trips, and important relationships._____
_____
_____

3. Include important quotations, books, movies, and music which exemplify values you identify with._____
_____
_____

People in your life. Thank influential people, express regrets to anyone you may have hurt. (See the Fourth Step in the AA Program, i.e., make amends)_____
_____
_____

4. Last words, quips for the tombstone, memorial, or urn._____
_____
_____

5. Write a goodbye poem. _____
_____
_____
_____

Suicide Note: For some reason, I'm reluctant to write this today, having worked on a crisis hotline at Health and Welfare in Boise, Idaho during my training as a Clinical Social Worker. Some individuals are "Para suicidal," that is, they make gestures of suicide to prevent others from abandoning them. Others are seriously suicidal, and they have usually tried before, they have a plan currently, and they exhibit behaviors, such as giving away important things, changing a will secretly, or writing their actual goodbye note.

There are some individuals with diagnoses of Histrionic or Borderline Personality Disorder for whom suicidal gestures are coping mechanisms, ways of preventing relationships from ending or for whom the ER in the local hospital is seen as a desirable place to be. There is another type who romanticizes the act of suicide as a logical end for a person with Existentialist ideas, or someone who glamorizes the deaths of Curt Cobain, Janice Joplin, Jimi Hendrix, or from an earlier era, poets and writers, such as Virginia Woolfe.

Individuals with Bipolar I Disorder and Major Depressive Disorder suffer some of the worst depressions imaginable. I would say someone with either of these diagnoses should skip this exercise and move on. For people going through adjustment neuroses, think of this as an extreme exercise in the process of the therapist "shaking the client's tree" to bring up feelings.

Suicide Note: There are three stages in crisis work with suicidal clients. The first stage is to completely listen to the person and his or her complaints. The second stage is to begin helping the person look for reasons to live. The third is to make a contract with the person so that they will not hurt themselves, they will not drink or use (more) drugs, they will contact someone and not be alone any more, and they will hand over any weapons, pills, knives, hoses or ropes with which they could hurt themselves.

Begin writing by free-associating around recent events which have caused you to re-experience earlier abandonment issues from your childhood, which resulted in job losses, financial problems or physical health issues. Imagine the worst that could happen. You should unequivocally "whine" and complain for as long as necessary without self consciousness. If your problems are financial, imagine living on the streets or in your car. Imagine life without your spouse, girlfriend or boyfriend, your current job or lifestyle, a record contract, your deceased family member or partner. Take it all the way out. Imagine the humiliations of bankruptcy, loss of status, shame of your friends' seeing you at a complete loss, and imprisonment. Imagine horrendous trauma, victimization, disfigurement, concentration camps, even physical pain. Then see if you would give up your life, even if you are facing a life sentence in prison. Can you imagine yourself "not being here," alive on this planet? Begin writing.

_____
_____
_____
_____
_____
_____
_____

COMING OF AGE

A COMING OF AGE STORY FOR AMERICAN ADOLESCENTS: AUTHOR'S SHORT STORY USED TO ILLUSTRATE ADOLESCENT IDENTITY AND BOUNDARY ISSUES

This piece is about being an adolescent male during the sixties. After I left high school, I had dreams about this coach depicted in the story, for almost two years. The life events, which precipitated the story, are common with males and females now because of Title IX, except for the twist in the middle of the story. It deals with the themes of marriage, passage into the first phase of adulthood, identity development, sexuality, and social roles and the manipulations of adults trying to gain something from the teen who is moving on.

Symbolically, depth of field is a photographic reference which describes the power of the lens to capture a certain amount of territory, according to how open or shut the lens is. The more open it is, the less depth of field you have; the more closed it is, the further you see. The play on the word field also gives it a double meaning, which is the terrain on which games are played.

DEPTH OF FIELD, BY STEVE FLICK

"Marks," screamed coach Beattie, "in my office!"

Marks tightened the towel around his waist and walked to the dark end of the locker room where he poked his head just past the door and said, "What's up, coach?"

"Work on some weights this spring and go out for track. If you can take a couple of tenths off your hundred time, I might just be able to get you a scholarship."

"I'll think about it," said Marks, "but I love my knees coach. I might just play baseball." He was aware of studying coach Beattie too long. Beattie liked to wear white, short-sleeved shirts and clip-on ties. Legend had it that Omar Braxton, class of 57, had grabbed a real tie once and nearly killed Beattie after an argument with coach. Marks looked to the coach's left at Weirman, coach's nerdy assistant. This year, 1960, it was Weirman. His horned-rim glasses trapped the steam and funneled it down the lenses and onto the front of his shirt. The nerd was always a nark, and you couldn't say or do anything in earshot of said nark, or you'd hear about it Monday at the team meeting. The narks seemed OK sacrificing their cool for the power they got from the adults.

"I already sent out your tapes to six northwest school weeks ago," he said, "you should hear from them soon. Now get out of here."

Marks backed out of the office and returned to his locker, relieved he hadn't told coach about his trip to San Francisco to meet the baseball coach. Marks and his dad Ray had brought the album full of clippings from his junior year when he'd gone ten and one as a pitcher and hit .450 with some power. He'd played in the American Legion All Star game that summer at first base behind the hard-throwing Strindberg who had a 90-mile-an-hour fast ball. Strindberg had been signed by the Cubs and was playing rookie ball in Idaho. Marks had planned to go to Tahoe to bus dishes with five guys on the team. It was a tradition that senior letter carried on when they graduated, staying in the cabin of a famous alumni.

As a senior Marks came to training camp having grown from 5'10" to 6'2" during the summer. He'd added twenty pounds and came back to practice at 195. Only one guy could beat him in the 40 and that was Eddie Mandel, but Mandel slowed down with the pads on, and Marks did not.

Marks snapped himself out of his reverie, dressed, and began the walk home. Soon, Brad Hartung pretended to try and run him over on the radiant sidewalk, stopping his Barracuda within inches of his leg, the nose of the car over the curb. When Marks got in and said thanks, Hartung said, "Slumber party, this weekend, the foothills, bring your sleeping bag and your own booze!" He dragged out all the words, trying to sound official. Marks shook his head and looked south at the bay where the road lifted the car out of downtown. The water was green today, not much foam down by the rocks, and two tankers passed each other out by the old ferry dock. He remembered one summer day with Hartung after they had built a huge raft with telephone poles and a plywood deck, getting stuck beyond the jetty when the tide came in.

Hartung thought he was a ladies' man, but someone had told him that women liked the natural scent of a man; unfortunately, Marks thought Hartung stank like sliced onions in the car. Marks got out and thanked him for the ride. He walked down the driveway into his flat-roofed, tract home and entered from the carport. "Hey mom, I'm home," he yelled. Susan Marks greeted her son with a hug. She treated every day he came home from practice uninjured as a gift from God. She checked his arms, back and face for defects. Marks noticed the hamburger, peas, French bread and milk on the table, ready for dinner. Sue had ceased to be creative in the kitchen once his father had taken the swing shift job at the paper.

"I'll never be able to eat another pea when I leave this house," he said."

"I'll never cook another one," said Sue. After a pause she said, "You got a phone call from the Oregon State football scout. He wants to come over later this week."

"Coach said he's sent out film to six schools up north." Marks began to eat. He could taste the salty meat triggering his saliva glands. He ate meat, bread, peas, and washed them down with milk. The thought of someone telling him what to do for another four years upset him. "Can we afford State U. in the City?" he asked.

"If you bus dishes at Tahoe and save your money," she said. "I'm glad you don't want to play football," Sue continued. "I couldn't worry for another four years. I invited the scout over just so we could hear what he had to say. Just so you can explore your options. It could be entertaining."

To him it was a choice between living in another small town or going to a big, cosmopolitan city, Corvallis or San Francisco. His dad would be mad, but he always went along in the end. "If that's what you want, son," he'd say, "then that's what I want." Marks watched some TV; then, he got out the 34" bat and began to practice his swing in front of the plate glass window, now darkened from the outside where the hasty sun slipped behind the Carquinez Bridge.

"I'll come back for a reunion a famous ball player," he thought. He flexed a bicep built up by pull-ups and chin-ups he'd done in the summer. He turned on the blues station from Oakland and shut the door to the TV where his mom watched Hallmark Theater. "The mirror is the garden of dreams," he thought, then wrote in his small, black, daily diary.

He thought it was weird that he stared in the mirror so much, the way he saw the girls do unselfconsciously every day at school. It was a circuit he had to test constantly, not remembering if he had remained attractive since the last time he'd look, thinking some leprosy had bloomed in the interim. He moved from the bat to the radio to the diary in quick intervals because each activity stimulated some other need for activity in his brain.

At ten he kissed his mom goodnight and climbed into his twin bed. He opened the window and listened to the wind move against the furniture in the patio, shushing the sheets, rustling the umbrella, urging the hanging wooden chimes which clashed once and then just swung wildly in a tangle. He removed his underwear and masturbated, thinking of Julie Ashley, the school sex object. When he was done, he put the fluid in a Kleenex on the floor under the bed and felt relieved and guilty at the same time. Some priest had told him and his old girlfriend Kelly a really sordid story about two teenagers who died in a car after having sex and had gone straight to hell. His dad hated Catholics, and he knew what a mound of crap that kind of hell was. Hell was your own psyche, dad said, the Bible is a set of metaphors but not a set of instructions to be taken literally. The Catholics could do anything, they just had to feel guilty about it and confess and go to heaven. How did everyone get so serious about this shit, he wondered, you can't prove any of it. Look around: my dog died last summer. I dug it up and it was still there a year later, eaten by maggots, the maggots had fed the birds, the birds made a nest, their babies took off, and there you go.

Marks slept and dreamed a teenage dream of anxiety, including classrooms, missing homework, angry adults transformed into monsters chasing him to the elevator where he knew the wires would break and he would wake up in the morning, sweating, his heart jumping like a pigeon.

The next day he daydreamed of Julie Ashley and looked up the encyclopedia's definition of auburn, the color of her hair. It was a moderate brown that is yellower and duller than toast brown, lighter and slightly yellower than tobacco, paler and yellower than bay, redder and slightly stronger then coffee. He had passed within touching distance of her in the hall and inhaled the scent of her Charly as he walked toward the dressing room. He turned to look at her, and he glimpsed her turn her head just sideways enough to see if he'd looked.

Marks, in the humid hotness of the bayside town, circa 1960, the year birth control pills went on the market and the country went haywire, lined up, facing the area bounded by two tackling dummies, dressed in his white, grass-stained practice uniform. Jimmy Barrett was his partner, about six feet tall, 175 pounds and solid, a kid with pimples pumped into him by his crippled and domineering old man.

Marks saw green stains on Barrett's knees before bending over in his three-point stance on that day of first full-contact drills. Marks was scared and tasted dry metal in his mouth. "She's got the sweetest auburn hair," he mused. Coach Beattie blew the whistle, startling Weirman next to him. Marks lunged for the no-man's land between the dummies…something was wrong, Marks knew, for all he could see was grass. He tried to get his head up, but it was too late. The back of his head took a couple of hard-driving knees, and in seconds he had become a new individual who didn't have or know a name.

They said he had wandered around, dazed for several minutes, without knowledge of his name, without knowing where his locker was, without a combination, without knowledge of his teammates. Weirman and he shared a brief moment of compassion for each other in coach's office while Weirman went though the card file and found his numbers. Marks was repeating the phrase, "Poor mommy, poor mommy," like a retarded parrot. The blow had dislodged the phrase, which reflected the main preoccupation of his life, trying to make his mother feel better. It was as though he had become delayed in that instant, and all of his memories, identity and future had disappeared.

When he came to in Kaiser Hospital, all that remained was a headache. He couldn't remember why he was there, and the past day had been erased from his consciousness. The doctor who was examining him had large pock marks from childhood smallpox. Doc sat on the edge of the bed, trying to calm Sue marks. "It's a class three concussion from which he should probably never show any effects. It probably affected your mother more than you," he said, "try to keep your head up during tackling drills from now on." Marks smiled and looked at his mother. Perhaps she'd thought he'd be delayed for life, instead of just a day, walking around the house babbling, "Poor mommy, poor mommy."

When they went home, his dad was up, wearing his mangy, pink bathrobe, and they sat down for a family conference. "A football scout from Oregon State called," he said, "I told him to come up tonight so you could meet him."

"He's not playing football," Sue said.

"Why not? Just because of some concussion? Sue, it'd really help us out if he got a scholarship."

"We can afford to send him to San Francisco State if we both keep working and he works summers," she said.

"Is that what you want?" he said, looking at his son. Marks nodded his head. "Well then, you guys listen to the scout and tell him you're going to State. I'm glad you're OK, it was frightening, listening to you stuck like a phonograph saying 'Poor mommy, poor mommy' all afternoon."

"I told you this was dangerous," Sue said, raising her voice as his dad. Then, she began to cry.

Sue drove him to school with her makeup smudged from the tears. She wore a navy A-line skirt and a silk blouse. Marks wore his good shirt, Levis, and penny loafers. He felt as if he had experienced a death and had come back to tell about it. Coach said he didn't have to practice for the rest of the week. Between classes he saw Julie Ashley and asked her to go to the A&W that afternoon. He wondered where he'd gotten the courage. She seemed surprised and said, "I'll call my mom after firth period to have her pick me up there. I heard you went dingy for a day?"

"Yeah, I don't remember anything except your perfume when you walked by me," he joked.

"You remember that," she said, "it was Charly." They said the three words simultaneously.

The scout from Oregon State wore a brown suit, blue tie, and white socks which he tried to hide when he crossed his legs. Marks and Sue sat on the big couch perpendicular to the fireplace, facing the plate glass window overlooking the bay. The scout sat facing them, his back to the view. Marks wasn't sure why they had worked him over so badly, but the scout was paying for all the waste, stupidity, and regimentation he and his family had endured for football. For some reason he sat and took it.

"Your college doesn't have a sociology major," Marks almost shouted, "that's what I want to study. How can I go somewhere when they don't have the major I want."

"I think we're getting one soon because it's a pretty popular major. By the way, we want to move you to split end instead of tight end because of your speed and hands. Didn't you run a 10.2 in a track meet? We think you can block and catch out there. Out split ends have to catch and block," he said lamely. "Congrats on the Chronicle nomination," he continued. "We are signing 13 players from the first four Chronicle All-Star teams to come to Corvallis. You'll be in good company." Marks felt the flattery soften his resistance. He thanked the man and offered him some coffee and angel food cake. They munched quietly, making sucking sounds with the coffee, making small talk.

"Gotta' hit the pillow and drive home tomorrow," he said, shaking hands with Marks and Sue. "Here's my card," said the scout, "I'll be in the Bay Area for another week signing guys, and I'll call you before I drive back if you change your mind. I'll tell the baseball coach you might want to walk on. That might work out. Then we could talk you into some football."

Marks was exhausted at trying to negotiate his future as an adult. "I love my knees, coach, but thanks for coming up here and spending your time." Sue and Marks watched him back out the driveway. Then Sue turned on him.

"I saw you with Julie Ashley at the A&W today," Sue said, "I thought you were supposed to rest?" She had that raspy edge on her voice when her anger got stuck there. He turned to reply, remembering how Julie had ignited the whole left side of his body, just sitting there next to him in the booth. "You know, some people say she's the school slut…she comes from people I don't want you to be seen with. Do you want to be stuck in this town forever with a trailer-trash wife? I don't want you to see her any more."

"Who said she was a slut?" he bellowed, "you don't even know what a slut is right now, it's been so long for you." Marks had so much adrenaline in his upper body he started trembling. "Julie's just the most popular babe in school, the best looking, the smartest, she's going somewhere. I don't know where you get your gossip, but you're completely off base. Someone's jealous and daydreaming she's a slut."

They glared at each other, standing in the living room, surrounded by teacups and cake crumbs. When Sue saw him shaking, she turned her head, backed away and sat down. "You shouldn't be showing affection in public," Sue said.

"Why, because you and dad aren't?" he shot back at her. "I'll put my arm around anybody I want. What do you think, this is Victorian England? Jesus!"

"That was cruel." She stood up as if to slap him, but he caught her forearm and gripped it so hard her skin squeaked.

"I'm almost out of this stupid town," he said, "this stupid school." He coughed from rage and felt his genitals shrivel. "Sometimes I think you and dad are stupid for living this way. You moved into separate bedrooms when we moved up here. Didn't you think I'd notice? It's 1960, ma, you and dad don't love each other, but that's not my problem. Don't blame that shit on me and tell me not to show Julie affection. That's your hang-up."

"I'm sorry," she said, a little shaken, "you're just acting like this because of your concussion. You've never talked this way to me before."

"You've never tried to control me like this before. Nobody really talks about anything around here, not since dad went on nights." He walked out into the cool dark evening and stood there looking at their newly built tract home. When he turned, he could see a huge oil tanker being pushed sideways by tugboats at either end of the tanker, into the fuel dock across the straits where the oil was siphoned off and jet fuel was stored in the tanks high on the hill across the bay for the Air Force. He knew he'd go back inside and make up because he always went first.

He remembered the campout drinking party Hartung had told him about, and Marks decided at that moment he was going. He was tired of always being the one to walk the drunks around and do their paper routes. This time he was going to puke his guts out and let them hold him up. He would stand outside Julie's house and howl at the moon, tell her how much he loved her and make a total fool of himself. Inside, he found Sue crying and wiping her eyes. "I'm sorry we fought ma," he said contritely, "you never said anything about my dating girls like that before."

"She was just so pretty, son. I am ashamed. I was jealous of you, sitting there in the A&W with your lives all in front of you. You've turned out to be someone I'm proud of, and I don't want anything bad to happen to you. You're my family. The way you walked around here saying, 'Poor mommy, poor mommy' I thought you were permanently brain-damaged. And I would have to take care of you for the rest of your life. Then, next thing I know, you were well and I saw you with her, and I felt all alone."

"I'm leaving next fall, so I have to start doing what I need to do. So do you."

"Who knows anymore," Sue said.

"Mom, you're supposed to know," he said, "you're the parent. It's my job to go away. It's yours to know what you want. That's what all that practice is about." He kissed her on the top of her head. He went to the liquor cabined and grabbed a flask-sized pint of whiskey and put it down into his underwear. "I'm going to a senior slumber party, mom. Nobody's driving, and we're all sleeping over. It's chaperoned, so I won't be home until Sunday morning, capiche?" She nodded and turned on the TV. There was a knock at the door. Marks opened it and there was Coach Beattie, hands in his pockets, feet shifting back and forth under him.

"Coach," Marks barked, "what are you doing here?"

"The OSU coach called me and said you're not interested in the scholarship. You know chances like this don't come around to everybody, you know, some people get opportunities and don't take advantage…" Marks went through the open door, motioning for coach to follow him, and as he did, he smelled alcohol.

With the door closed Marks said, "I told you I wasn't going to play football in college...I love my knees." It was hard to get a breath. This time coach had gone too far.

"You know what I would have given to play on scholarship somewhere? It was the concussion, wasn't it? That's what's stopping you. You're scared ever since you got the lights knocked out. I would have given anything to play on scholarship somewhere."

"Coach, you told us you did play at Seattle University." Marks remembered the orientation where they showed the film of his dog outrunning all the referees during a game. The memory stabbed him like a harpoon.

"I'm not you coach. I might walk on and play baseball, I might actually study something and learn how to write or be a sociologist. I already made up my mind."

Beattie took two steps back down the driveway and said, "You know Marks, you were always out for yourselves. You never were a team player." Saliva stuck on one side of his mouth in a string. Marks lifted his fists and took two steps out onto the carport when the bottle came out of his pants leg, shattering on the concrete. His mother walked toward him from the family room, asking who was there.

Coach stumbled backwards, waving his arms, turned and lurched to the street.

"What's the matter?" Sue said.

"Everybody wants something, now that I'm leaving."

"We should have sent you to that little Quaker school in Canada," she said quietly. "You could stay there and not worry about the draft." She helped him clean up the glass and cheap whiskey, and she never asked him why.

ANALYZE THE STORY DEPTH OF FIELD USING THE FORMAT: WRITE OUT ANY OF YOUR OWN ISSUES THAT RELATE TO THE CHARACTERS IN THE STORY

If you are doing this story out loud in a group, assign two or three clients to each concept of literature, for example plot, setting, character, style, theme and gut level reaction. Get a definition of each concept, and have the groups do an analysis focusing only on the concepts for their group. Remember, a good story is like an iceberg, and just as a therapist goes under water to bring the unconscious of the client to the surface, when you analyze a good story or a good movie you do the same thing.

Things to watch for: what events are taking place outside the story that affect the character and his family? What changes occurred in the character after the concussion?

What psychological issues cause conflict for the 18-year-old Marks between himself and his school, his family, internally, and his identity? Why would an author use a teen's last name only in a longer story like this? What is the symbolism (what does name represent) of the word "marks" on all its different levels? What role does Marks play in his family?

Here are the concepts used in the analysis of a short story or novel. Plot: Summary in a paragraph, conflict, climax, coincidence, suspense, surprise, foreshadowing. Look up these words in a collegiate dictionary and write out their definitions.

Setting: physical setting or environment (time and place), social setting or milieu (social class of characters), identification of setting, significance of setting, setting shift, expectations of setting, overt or covert meanings of setting.

Character: Characters are the people in fiction as presented by the author. It is broken into makeup, motivation, moral values, conflicts and problems, character change, lifelike or real. Character is revealed in these ways: directly and indirectly. Does the character change within his or her possibilities? Is it motivated by circumstances? Does it occur within a believable length of time? How does character reveal the themes of the author?

Style: The elements of style are point of view, language, atmosphere (mood and tone). Point of view tells us whose story it is. It refers to the eyes and mind through which actions are seen. Point of view is reflected also in whether the story is told in first person, second person, or third person points of view.

Language: There are eight aspects of this facet of style. Look up the definitions in a good dictionary and work from there. They are diction, syntax, imagery, symbolism, irony, paradox, ambiguity, and allusions.

Atmosphere: this consists of mood and tone. Mood is the emotion called forth in the reader. Tone (of voice) is the author's attitude toward the subject and the reader. Adjectives which describe tone include objective, serious, humorous, sarcastic, tragic, etc.

Theme or Unifying Idea: This is the main idea concerning the comment made overtly or covertly by the author about the experience created in the literary work. My equation or shorthand for this is content=theme. What is contained in the story reveals its theme.

It's obvious to me as a therapist, teacher and writer, that the author's own inner dialog, perception of character and human behavior, and imprinting a theme upon his or her works involve highly sophisticated understanding of psychology. One aspect of fiction is to help a reader "see through" the iceberg to the unconscious basis of human life. Analyze the story using the concepts of literature.

_____

_____

_____

_____

_____

_____

_____

_____

WRITING ABOUT THE 12 STEPS OF AA/NA

I have always been fascinated with the fourth and fifth steps of AA/NA, mostly because the writing here revolves around a "personal inventory" and "making amends" where it will not hurt the individual one is making amends to. It is a combination of the confessional and directly searching for forgiveness. The Fourth Step says, "Made a searching and fearless moral inventory of ourselves" (*The 12 Steps: A Way Out*, Friends in Recovery). In this way, writing out the fourth step is where the alcoholic/addict confronts the truth about himself and what he/she did. Drugs and alcohol basically are first and foremost, pain-killing agents. By using them, the addicts prevent themselves from developing coping mechanisms to deal with challenges in their real lives, to deal with the pain of everyday life; they prevent themselves from growing up. When addicts stop using, they are basically the same age they were when they began. They don't know how to express feelings (not "racket" emotions to gain attention or to divert their associates away from their use), be parents, hold a job, go to school, and be in a relationship. The "flow" they generated was generated by substances, not by their own adrenaline, endorphins, serotonin, L-Dopa, all which are produced naturally in the brain. The addict has lots of experience dealing with flow created by substances. He is an expert, says Patrick Carnes.

1. Resentment_____

2. Fear_____

3. Repressed or inappropriately expressed anger_____

4. Approval seeking_____

5. Caretaking of others_____

6. Control_____

7. Fear of abandonment_____

8. Fear of authority figures_____

9. Frozen feelings_____

10. Irresponsibility_____

11. Isolation_____

12. Low self-esteem_____

13. Overdeveloped sense of responsibility_____

14. Inappropriately expressed sexuality_____

15. Character strengths (the inventory includes positives as well as negatives)_____
_____

Carnes in his workshop materials has offered some amazing synthesis which blends addiction theory and behavior with Csikszentmihalyi's concepts of "Flow." The recovering addict, he says, needs to learn how to create "flow" in new ways, through retraining him or herself to tune into the adrenaline available in every day life, such as through the body, watching children grow up, creating art and writing, having control over self, learning, and relating.

Try this: Take a searching and fearless moral inventory of yourself (or your client can do this). Use these following subheadings to describe negative emotions or patterns which hold you back from having a successful life.

Step Five: Admitted to God, (I prefer Yoda or the Life Force) to ourselves, and to another human being the exact nature of our wrongs. The fifth step listener can be a member of a Twelve-Step program, a clergyman, a trusted friend, doctor, psychologist, a family member, a counselor or therapist.

"SCENE FROM AN NA MEETING" FROM *TELLER'S LAST BAND,* BY STEVE FLICK

Most counselors and therapists have never been to an AA or NA open meeting before. Earlier in my career as a Psychiatric Aide, I was able to accompany clients to a nightly meeting which took place in the psychiatric facility in which I worked. The following scene is a work of fiction distilled from those experiences, and appears in my novel *Teller's Last Band*, Writer's Club Press, 2002. In this scene, Teller and Alan Bristowe, the rock star, attend an NA meeting together, and the woman who is running the meeting tells her story with so much truth, it is stunning to Teller, and causes Bristowe to begin his own rehabilitation.

"Scene from an NA Meeting"

Dr. Girdstein shook his head as he looked at the X-rays and Alan Bristowe's test results. Bristowe leaned like a little boy off the sides of the examination table, swing his feet back and forth. "You're got to come back," the doctor said, "You've lost some liver function, your kidneys appear to be infected, your spleen is enlarged, ostensibly from drug use—am I right? Heroin?"

Bristowe nodded. "Everything, really," he said.

"...And your platelet count is a little high. I'd like to start you on some medication as soon as possible—but I've seen worse. You don't have anything we can't fix with some sane living. You have impotence due to a malfunction in your prostate, and it appears you have some rectal problems...but I'm not sure why." Bristowe and Teller looked at each other, then quickly back at the doctor. "How soon can you come in?"

"Well, tomorrow morning I can bloody well come in," Bristowe said in character, "I'll cancel everything, cancel the goddamned day, make the sun stay down." He took the champagne he had put against the wall, stood up and poured it into the doctor's wash basin. "The body is the end of all excess isn't it? The biophysical limit of it all...the herpes, the AIDS, the viruses, the Ebola, the drugs."

On the exam room walls were pictures of the Doc riding a wind sail, finishing the Triathlon in Hilo, and boxing with a middle-weight in a local Kalihi gym. "A bloody health nut," Bristowe muttered. "They don't understand that as an artist, you're sacrificing your bloody body because you have to perform in front of thousands of people."

"This doctor has to perform, and he doesn't sacrifice his body," Teller said. "Doc, I never knew you were into all this stuff."

"You'll notice I was a lot younger," Girdstein said.

"The good doctor doesn't have to see 13 cities in a month to perform. He has all of medicine to draw from; he doesn't have to draw from his creativity."

"You're just rationalizing your substance abuse," Teller said, "you must feel threatened."

"You sound like a chemical dependency proselyte," Bristowe said.

"You're young, you'll recover this time, but if you let it go too much longer, there might be permanent damage. Could you gentlemen write me that check now? This is irregular...I had to persuade a couple of technicians to get the lab work done."

"Sure Doc," Bristowe said, putting on his shirt. He leaned out the door and told Dan Orr to write the check. "Thanks a heap, Doc. I'll see you in the morning."

"Would you sign this CD cover for my daughter?" Doc asked.

Bristowe signed, and they walked out of the office toward the front door. Just before they reached the exit, Bristowe noticed a room full of people who sat in a brightly-lit, smoke-filled room. "What's that?" he asked.

"It's the NA meeting, I think," Teller said.

"Let's go," Bristowe commanded. He turned toward the light and straightened as if about to go on stage. Orr and Teller followed him to the back of the room. Thick smoke and coffee smells made Teller slightly ill. There were new rugs and chairs in the room, which had a large plate glass window, offering a view of the small valley which ran east to the mountain. A large video screen and a movie projector were the focus of the gathering while an aluminum canister of coffee burbled in the haze of cigarette smoke. Teller saw a one-armed man with a pirate face, several younger men and women, dressed as if they'd just come from their jobs downtown. At the front of the group, sitting on a stool was a woman who ran the meeting.

Annice was a pretty, pixie-like woman. "Hi, I'm Annice, and I'm a drug/addict/alcoholic/sex addict/nicotine fiend/social misfit." The group said hello to Annice. She was so short, she had to point her toes to lower her foot far enough for it to reach the floor. She had brown hair tied in a ponytail, wide eyes, and she wore Levi's which showed her round bottom, her round calves; she was round all over.

"Tonight," she went on, "we have an open meeting for people who might consider joining, so we must repeat that anything said in this room is confidential, and the group must decide if we're to let new members in on this night. What are your names please?"

Teller felt awkward. He imagined what he might say. "Hi, my name is Don. I'm a neurotic. I've got 'brown-womanitis.' I'm addicted to music, TV and food. I've left my wife and son, and I'm about to be famous. I'm the son of a preacher man…PKs anonymous."

Bristowe was braver. "Hello, I'm Alan, and I'm addicted to rock 'n roll." The group laughed. "And I'm here because my friend told me about it, and I want to see if I'm a bloody drug addict/alcoholic like you all say."

"I'm Dan, "Orr said, "I was at one time a junkie, but I kicked with the help of my wife."

"You recovered," Annice said, "you're a recovering addict. You'll always be an addict."

"That's right, ma'm" Orr said, quietly sitting down.

"My name is Don," Teller said, I'm a counselor here on the psychiatric units."

"Welcome to the group," Annice said. "I'm here to talk about the voice behind the game of drug peddling. I've peddled my ass, I've peddled my possessions, my clothes, my family, my mind, my jobs, my ex-husband and my self respect. We used to live in Maui when I was a practicing addict." Teller noticed a slight lisp from her overbite.

"My first wife—shit, what a Freudian slip!—my first life was as a working woman, wife, member of the community. My second life involved a relationship with a heavy user of cocaine, a dealer on Maui. For taking drugs to buyers for him, I received a small cut of whatever I carried. One night I got greedy, but the buyer noticed." The members of the group grew silent and leaned forward, listening to her story. "He got out a .357 Magnum and stuck it in my face. He made me have sex with him for several hours to pay for what was missing. In the process, he gave me so much cocaine that I nearly died. My heart was palpitating so fast. My dealer got worried about me; so did my ex-husband. They both showed up at the yacht where I was being held captive. All of them showed up at the same time, each with a gun pointed at someone else. There I was naked, three guns in a room, a large amount of coke on the table. I'm almost dead, and they're shouting at each other.

" 'Men,' I said, 'would someone call an ambulance? I think I'm dying. You can shoot it out later.' I was terrified. My spouse took me to the hospital where they gave me more drugs, and I went into a coma."

Teller couldn't reconcile her pixie presence with her degrading tale. He looked to see what was so beautiful about her. She talked about her feelings in a way he had never heard. She talked about the terrors she had lived as if she were describing cleaning a house. She asked for no response, made no apology, did not try in any way to elicit sympathy.

"When I got out of the hospital, my husband had packed his things and moved back to the Mainland. I had to move into my pusher's place, having no place to go." She spoke without neurotic laughter or modification. "I lost twenty pounds. I developed a nasal condition and started turning tricks in the hotels…not because of the nasal condition."

They laughed. Teller saw the way she wrapped one leg around the back of the other, the weight of which was supported by one toe. The lisp made it hard to believe the story could have happened to her. It was like discovering that Tinkerbelle had given VD to Peter Pan, Wendy, the dog, and Captain Hook.

"Drugs were my life. I began to think of ways to kill myself. I stole. I was going down and down, and somewhere in the down, I hit bottom. One night in the Maui Hilton they had a convention of AA and NA members. I was hoping to drum up some extra business. I was sick and tired of being sick and tired. I thought I'd slip in and pick up a couple of johns. People were telling their stories, just the way I am telling you mine tonight, and I began thinking there was some way out, other than killing myself. They played a tape of a man who spoke at the national conference in LA several years ago."

"Bobby B.," said the man with the pirate face.

"Yeah, Bobby B.," Annice said. "He spoke of the vulture beside his bed every morning when he woke up, the vulture which told him that each day was shit, that he was shit, and that there wasn't any point to living. When I heard that, I knew it was my vulture too, and that I had to start looking at what was going on in my life. I stood up and asked for help. It was like one of those tent meetings where the people come up asking to be saved. Well, I stood there asking to be saved. I got a sponsor that night who got me into detox and rehab. No one can help an addict until she's ready for it. The alcoholic/drug addict has one chance in ten of helping herself. There are fifteen million hard-core addicts and ten percent get help. The rest just ruin their lives, die, kill others, go to jail, and slough out of society.

"Those Maui members got me started on four years of sobriety—drug-free years, the best years of my life. My husband moved back to the islands, so I can see my baby, but I hurt him too badly to continue being married. You know what they say. Alcoholics don't have relationships, they take hostages. He didn't want to be a hostage." There were tears of loss in her eyes then. The group applauded when she was finished.

"I want to emphasize that this must be the center commitment of your life if you want to change. The way you know that is if you're a sponsor and your member lies to you about his or her drinking, you let them go. Recovering addicts should not have opposite sex relationships for at least a year from a "birthday." The reason is there's no point to exploring anything else but complete abstinence from nearly every drug. Besides, we would just move from getting high off drugs to getting high off a relationship.

"Some of us go all the way down to jail, tissue damage, relationship damage, killing someone with a car, almost getting killed in a deal, disease, degradation. Whatever you do, don't enable someone to continue drinking by some misguided notion of help. The sooner they hit bottom, the sooner they'll make the decision to quit, and they won't have taken you with them.

"Just tell yourself, 'Just for today, I'll focus on my recovery. Just for today I'll have faith in NA. I'll find people who aren't using and who have a new way of life. I don't have to understand what made me this way, like the shrinks say, but I do understand how to stop using and change my life. Then, some day I'll understand how I got here.'"

"The last thing is to remember that you and I are now, have been, and always be alcoholic/drug addicts, who will never, ever again be able to stand around at some cocktail party and drink two glasses of wine, or two martinis, or two beers or two of anything, and to go home with a buzz on. One drink or a thousand, we will always be alcoholics/drug-addicts, recovering one day at a time."

"Amen," said a man in front of Teller. Annice closed her eyes. Someone opened the *Big Book* and three members each read a paragraph. Teller looked at Bristowe and Orr. Bristowe looked shaken. They all stood in line to thank Annice after the meeting. Bristowe had hung a beige, Gucci suit over his thin frame; underneath was a silk shirt, orange like soda pop. He wore loafers with no sox. A matching orange kerchief peeked over the top of his left pocket. He shook her hand, said a few words and motioned for Orr and Teller to follow him out the door. No one asked for Bristowe's autograph.

"Can we drop you?" Bristowe said, dabbing his eyes.

"Glad that you came?" Teller asked.

"Got a lot to think about tonight," Bristowe murmured. Teller could smell the honeysuckle as they walked toward the limo in the parking lot. "We're doing a concert on the Big Island in a few weeks. It's going to launch our tour on the Mainland. I'm scared to stop using before I go on the road. I don't know if I can do it."

"Get someone to talk to about it. Go back in there and get the names of some people." Teller looked at Orr who stared at Bristowe, not believing what he was hearing.

Teller thought of Dustin with a pang of longing so strong, he thought he would have to lie down. He said goodbye and drove north to his apartment. In Kailua Bay and Kaneohe Bay he could see the booze cruise ships, the dinner sails, the boats just glimmering on the ocean past the breakers. He wanted to see and hold his son, something pure, something good. "If I made Dustin, I must be good," Teller thought. He drove on to his place where he fell asleep with his clothes on, his own words leaving him to sleep.

ANALYZE THE STORY

I have met very few counselors, therapists, psychologists or psychiatrists who have actually been to an AA meeting. The group or individual can read "Scenes from an AA Meeting and discuss it as though they were at a meeting. During an AA meeting, feedback is not necessarily given or asked for. The "story" is the lesson.

If the story is used in a more non-therapeutic context, have the members or individual see what aspects of the plot, setting, character, style and theme are being used in this story. Theme and character are the most common ways fiction concepts can be translated into therapeutic responses because everyone is responding to behaviors in a story and not real life. Here are some other uses to which the story may be put.
1. Use the story as an assessment tool to see if there is any underlying mental illness, such as bipolar disorder.
2. Compare the characters of Bristowe, Teller, and Annice, finding similarities and differences.
3. What aspects of the scene resemble an actual AA meeting and the principles used in AA?
4. How does the author try to show the contrast between the way Annice appears and her life experiences with cocaine?

Finally, "gut-level" responses of clients and students to fiction provide a therapist and the client with clues to their own attitudes and feelings about life. The major themes of "Scenes from an AA Meeting" revolve around sex, drugs, and rock'n'roll, three time-honored topics in our culture, especially among young people. Fiction gives enough of a context, so the readers can help decide for themselves if these lifestyles are productive or not, and it does it in a way that's non-judgmental. The doctor's feedback to Bristowe is mainly that the body is the biophysical limit of the sex, drugs, and rock'n'roll lifestyle, and it's up to Bristowe to decide what to do about it.

GROUP NARRATIVE (STORY) EXAMPLE OF A GROUP STORY STARTED BY THE AUTHOR

Group narration is a process used in Hollywood and New York to write TV, movies, and occasionally novels. I understand that authors such as Jackie Collins, for example, use a staff of writers to which she gives her ideas, and they develop them into scenes, critique, and pick the best ones. Novelists who write mysteries, romance, gothic novels and science fiction collaborate as a means of changing points of view or simply to stay motivated after many books. Decide if this example from an English 100 class has any potential for development.

This is an exercise in narration—story telling—a vital skill in therapy and beyond. Begin by writing the first paragraph of your story, book, soap-opera, etc., by introducing a character. Jean was a tall redhead who moved to Fiji to be in the Peace Corps. Or begin by describing a central conflict. Mike played tackle at Wilson High while his brother went to Jefferson. They had to face each other in the championship game because they attended different magnet schools. Or set a scene where the action takes place. Snoopy's opening line is as good as anything. "It was a dark and stormy night by the ocean. Barrett stared at the roiling sea, thinking of ending her life. She thought…"

This is a great "ice breaker" for group therapy because it allows the members to see how perverted the other participants are! You have five minutes to get your story off the ground. Then pass it to the person on the right of you. You will receive a first paragraph from the person on your left, and you must take the characters, the situation, the setting or conflict and continue the story begun by someone else. This takes a little bit longer, anywhere from 7-8 minutes. The leader signals when the time is up, and the papers get passed to the right. Then you have ten minutes to read the first two paragraphs and continue the story. Each time the story gets passes, you get an additional minute to read and continue the story. Continue this until there are a minimum of five long paragraphs and a maximum of eight. Finally, announce when the story must end and each member must bring the story to a resolution. You get your first paragraph back, and introduce yourself to the writer who got up to find you, the one who wrote the ending. You'll see what others have done to your original idea, and you'll confirm how demented and twisted the others are when you see what they did to your characters.

The group can look for models used in automatic story writing, plot twists and turns, character development, use of dialog, and potential for further writing.

"The Story of Bud"

When Bud knocked on the trailer door, he heard the sound of children running on carpet. A phlegm-filed voice said, "Who is it?"

"It's Bud Grant, your case worker." At least they answered today, he thought. "I've got some forms to fill out for Tiffany.

"Tiffany's sick—she's not going for that assessment thing."

"She has to go, Verleen, else the judge is taking everyone into foster care again."

After fire minutes, Tiffany slipped through the front door wearing tight shorts, a white shirt tied in a knot, showing bare skin, sandals, and an ankle bracelet.

(Writer #2) "So you think I had sex with Missy?" Bud blurted, "You know that could ruin my career?"

"Stuff your career with a sock," Tiffany said, "I know you're hot for me, you're just too uptight to do anything about it. Ah Bud," she continued wiggling towards him, her hands toying with the knotted shirt, you mad at me?" She looked up at him through dark lashes, coyly she said, "Why don't we forget that assessment, you know I could make you really happy."

Bud rolled his eyes. She was a voluptuous child of sixteen and always she teased him. He needed this job too much to give in but he always dreamed of Tiffany at night.

(Writer #3) She was the type of girl he would never have. Bud was your basic "Joe Six-pack," a civil servant maybe a touch too civil. A degree in philosophy from state had lead him to social work, and now Tiffany's door. Bam—a shot rang out. "Shit, what was that," Bud yelped.

Tiffany flew out the door and crushed into Bud. He caught her, not without noticing the knot had completely come undone on the already-too-small shirt.

(Writer #4) With the movement of his right hand, he could feel her firm, voluptuous breast fill his hand, his heart raced, and he could feel movement throughout his body, every body part twitched, he had no time to respond to his physiology, however, for at the same moment his maleness was moving, Missy fell through the screen door and all fell at him, blood splattering, bodies falling. He was dazed as he found himself on the ground, not with the soft warm breast of Tiffany, but with Missy's dead and bloody body. (END OF STORY)

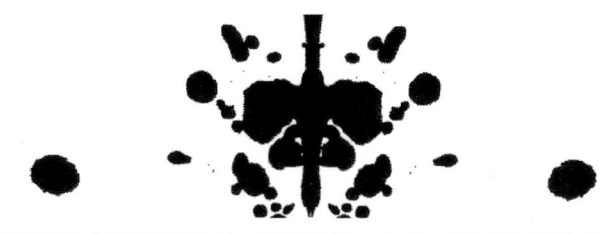

WRITING FOR CLIENTS WHO HAVE DEPRESSION

According to the *NIMH* pamphlet, 2005, "In any given one-year period, 9.5% of the population or about 30 million Americans, suffer from a depressive illness." Depressive illness often interferes with normal functioning. Depression involves the body, mood, and thoughts. It affects the way a person eats, sleeps, feels about self, and the way one thinks about things. The symptoms for depression include persistent sad moods, hopelessness, worthlessness, guilt, helplessness, loss of interest in activities that were once enjoyed, including sex, problems concentrating, insomnia and/or oversleeping, and thoughts of death or suicide (*NIMH* pamphlet, 2005, p. 3). A serious loss, difficult relationship, financial problem or any stressful change in life patterns can trigger a depressive episode. Depression, however, is one of the most treatable of the mental disorders, with 80% of those who receive medication, therapy or both, able to report significant improvements.

Approximately 40% of the Nobel Prize-winning poets during the past century were diagnosed with depression. It's clear, then, that the inner dialog which is the engine of depression is also the engine for much of the world's great writing! The connection seems obvious, put in those terms, so what do we do with it?

Writing of any kind can help the depressive person identify the thoughts and feelings which affect his or her moods. To that end, one has to learn how to "catch" the negative skull-rapping (Berne) which races through the mind of a depressed person.

The following exercise will help that person begin to see specifically what those self-talk messages are.

NEGATIVE COGNITIONS   POSITIVE COGNITIONS

I don't deserve love	I can have love
I am worthless	I am worthy
I am shameful	I am honorable
I am not good enough	I deserve good things
I cannot be trusted	I am trustworthy
I cannot trust my judgment	I can make good judgments
I cannot succeed	I can succeed
I am not in control	I am now in control
I am powerless	I now have choices
I cannot protect myself	I can learn to take care of myself
I am stupid	I have intelligence
I am insignificant	I am important
I am a disappointment	I am okay just the way I am
I deserve to die	I deserve to live
I cannot get what I want	I can get what I want
I have to be perfect	I can make mistakes
I am damaged	I can be healthy
I am ugly	I am fine
I should have done something	I did the best I could
I am in danger	It's safe now
I cannot stand it	I can handle it
I cannot trust anyone	I can choose whom to trust

Write about the negative thoughts (cognitions) first, because obviously those are the hardest to handle. Also, it's quite startling to listen to others' answers and to realize that many people are not aware of their own thoughts or skull rapping! We have 50,000 thoughts a day, as I've said before, and if one is depressed, most of them are negative. It's the function of the writing, the therapy, etc. to replace the negative thoughts from childhood as much as possible, to enable depressed people to move forward. That's why I see we need stories so much. We watch the characters overcome adversity, depression, challenges, and this gives us courage to keep working on own negativity.

Next, is a powerful exercise which never fails to produce strong feelings in the writer. It's very simple. As we carry our baggage from the past and process it during the day and during sleep, we unfortunately don't process the wonderful, positive things we have done, it's usually the negative scenarios from the past. It could be a divorce, failing in school, conflict with a loved one, a poor choice. As the scenarios invade the consciousness, let them roll out into the journal or computer.

Begin writing, "I forgive myself for……" over and over and over, finishing the sentence with the negative memory or scene.

I forgive myself for fighting with Sim.
I forgive myself for not getting my tenure.
I forgive myself for not supporting Diana when I should have.
I forgive myself for not being there more when my mom and dad were dying.
I forgive myself for having ADD and having trouble finishing my projects.

And so it goes. Now, you try.
The "I Forgive Myself" page.

_____
_____
_____
_____

HOW OLD ARE YOU, REALLY?

This exercise defined general age tasks that children typically engage in, according to research on development. In a sense, by openly identifying your true age, you are beginning to understand what the concept of "Inner Child" means. The concept of Inner Child arose from Eric Berne's Transactional Analysis, popularized by Harris in *I'm OK, You're OK* as a way of helping people in therapy locating the source of childhood feelings and fears. The Inner Child is characterized by feelings and fears, adapted (conforming), rebellious, and natural components. The natural child exhibits what he or she came into the world with, reflecting instinctual drives, spontaneity, as well as fears from total dependency. As you respond to the general age tasks in writing, you are looking for what feelings, behaviors and skills you have encompassed, and what you may still be working on. The numbers on the left represent the age the task is being exhibited.

1. Walking, speaking first words, exploring; all met with parental delight._____

2. Strides in motor and language; recognizes s/he is his or her own person, separate and distinct; asserts with negative._____

2 ½. Requires rituals, striving for control, zest for life, warmth and affection._____

3. Giving up some rituals and negatives, less resistant, more secure, longer attention span, nice plateau.
_____

4. Strive for freedom and independence, dress self, self-reliance at meals, less agreeable as they strive for greater freedom, "out of bounds" (boast, swear, kid,), imagination and creativity at all time high, very social, lively, exuberant, expansive, eager to meet new people, go to new places, learn.
_____

5. Interlude of harmony, less reaching out, more contentment, new level of maturity, more even temperament, quite skilled in small and large motor, can entertain self, preference for fantasy is being replace by interest in reality, appears calm, stable and more grown-up._____
_____

6. Outgoing age, eagerness to explore and learn, in a transition and still very self-centered; likes to be in charge and win, quick and wide mood swings.

7. Much more guilt that at age six, looking inward, "age of reason", absorbing, piecing together, making sense of, solidifying experiences, much more into observing, that introspection shows moodiness, states case in complaining tone, less bold, positive helpfulness, interest in sharing household chores.

8. Another action year, confidence up, cooperative, considerate, renewed faith in self to tackle world, pleasant to live with, moves steadily along, gaining skills in relating.

9. Continuation of age 8, self-confidence continues, increased independence, greater capacity to be a companion to friends and family, busy with self initiated projects, independent work, peers.

10. A climax, very positive about self and world, pride in family, enjoys them, typically likes position he is in, not a small child, not a teen, sheer delight, repeat of age five, harmony.

11. Last year of childhood, new stress and turmoil, emergence of teen years pressures, child unsettling, confusion of new thoughts and feelings can make child difficult to live with, can be argumentative and emotional outbursts, frequently feel picked on by parents, pattern for equilibrium/disequilibrium can be seen, rapid growth and stress, in adolescence the 12-14-16 years are smoother, 11-13-15 are more difficult.

12. Tends to be peaceful, friendly, easy going, gains pleasure in being taken more seriously, beginning to demonstrate s/he is not a child by more mature behavior.

13. Another significant about face occurs, new introspection emerges, often accompanied by a touchy nature, demands of seeking individuality produce anxiety, wants more privacy, can be quite sensitive to criticism.

14. Ease with teen years increases, as well as with personal evolution, more comfortable with social and psychological demands, sense of contentment increases.

15. As they get a closer view of adulthood, pangs of panic, fear of loss of childhood set in, they prepare for this by struggling for new freedoms and greater independence, more time with friends, less with family, less communicative._____

16. Reward again, renewed settling, high point of understanding and self-appreciation, doesn't need to fight for freedoms, more equal footing with adults._____

The are two age tasks which "live" in my inner child, even after living into my seniority: 1) The tasks which are listed in age seven 2) The tasks in age 13. When I took statistics in graduate school, I immediately turned in to a seven-year-old until it was over. Low tolerance for frustration began for me around that age. At 13, began the characteristic of being sensitive to criticism and refusal to try new things if I wasn't already good at them. Write a paragraph summarizing the general age task(s) you may still be engaged in.

_____
_____
_____

Writing enables the depressed person to cough up the contents of the self talk, and to begin having choices about how to respond to that negative self-talk, especially. For depressed persons, especially if they enjoy writing anyway, almost all of the previous exercises in this book will serve to help gain a perspective on a behavior which may seem normal before treatment, but which will eventually be defined as a symptom. One recent study found that regular, vigorous exercise alone was enough to enable 50% of clinically depressed people discontinue their medications!

_____
_____
_____
_____
_____

ANALYZE THE STORY

Sexual abuse, physical abuse, emotional abuse and neglect create adults who must rebuild their personalities without completing Erickson's first stage of Trust versus Mistrust. It creates depressed and confused adults. Suzanne Sgroi, M.D. writes about sexual abuse impact issues in her book *Handbook of Clinical Intervention in Child Sexual Abuse*. These are some of the primary ways CSA affects the lives of adults: Guilt, fear, depression, including suicidal ideation and self-mutilation, low self-esteem and poor social skills, "damaged goods" syndrome, anger and hostility, inability to trust, blurred role boundaries and role confusion, pseudo maturity and failure to complete developmental tasks, self-masking and control, drug and alcohol abuse.

In the story "The Play Room" Carrie is just beginning to make some headway with her behavior, just as mom and step dad separate, just as Carrie discloses. She needs the adults in her life to have completed their own developmental tasks, so they can help her repair her damaged boundaries. Carrie is a fictional client, but in general with real children it takes about six months of therapy (actually about 24 hours of counseling) before children will express undisclosed CSA. Some times the children protect the therapists from the gruesome details. There are so many symptoms from sexual and physical abuse that it's hard to use a "cookie cutter" approach to treatment.

For example, according to the PBS Broadcast *The Science of Murder* 52% of all convicted murderers relate a history of child abuse, and one study done at San Quentin revealed a much higher figure, 90%. According to one study, two-thirds of the women in prison for prostitution had been sexually abused (Silbert and Pines, 1981, cited in Arnold, 1990, p. 160). Current studies suggest that one of every three females in this country has experienced either molestation or intercourse as a child, and that one out of every six males has also the same experience.

Children who have experienced CSA, many times need regular old sex education because what has happened to them is so foreign and graphic, that it still may need explanation! A Christian mother of a 12-year-old male client, whose teen-aged step-brother had raped him, was insisting that the book I was using *What's Happening to my Body for Boys* was too explicit for her Christian beliefs. I had to explain that her son had already had a sexual experience and that he needed a straightforward depiction of what he had lived. Anything less would have been to deny the influence of this event on him. In this case the 12-year-old was worried that his step-brother would molest his little brother (6), and so he kept quiet about the sexual activity until the night that he was raped. In this case the behavior of protecting the little brother gave some meaning to why my client did not disclose sooner and also lowered the amount of guilt he felt about testifying in court and sending his step brother into treatment. Mother had also been sexually abused as a child, and her son's experience triggered her own impact issues as an adult. In her family life, however, she used Christianity to try and control her children and to defend against her own early sexual experiences.

THE PLAY ROOM

Glenn had rediscovered tennis after a ten-year absence. As he drove to Canyon City, listening to the jazz-fusion tape he and Carina made love to, he visualized the three sets he had played with Ray, his buddy. Ray was going with a woman whose father had sexually abused her, and Ray couldn't understand why she had problems in bed. Glenn remembered bits of dialog in his skull rapping as he headed towards the clinic, comments on the nature of love. "You are waiting for love from this woman as you waited for love from your mom. Don't call her therapist and muddle, it'll come back and bite you…don't quit your job…thoughts are bullshit, your feelings are the only compass, Ray." Ray had made him his therapist again. As he had gotten angrier, his shots picked up steam. He hit some crosscourt winners that Ray couldn't reach, and then Glenn's serve started to go in hard with just enough spin to be unreturnable.

It was the first time he'd beaten Ray in six months. They shook at the net, and Ray said, "What was that part about waiting?"

"You picked a wounded bird to save again," Glenn said, "next time you gotta' get someone who doesn't need fixing. You're picking women who bring up your family anger while you're waiting for them to love you. That's why it's so potent, so toxic." Ray went to his van, got a pen and paper and wrote down what Glenn said.

"I'm waiting…that's why I'm angry," he said. "I pick women who can't really love so I can get angry." *And, that's just their side of it. You attach so quickly you suck all of the space out of the relationship,* Glenn thought to himself.

Outside of Canyon City was a bridge from which daredevils parachuted and bungee jumped illegally. He phoned the office when he reached the main street, and Janelle answered. "Who's coming in today?" he said.

"Sherry Cowen, Mary Lou, the Edmonds', and Carrie Sanderson and her mother are here early waiting for you'all. You've got a full afternoon, and the men's group. Big day."

"Thanks," he said, "see you in a couple of minutes."

The play room is lit like a stage today, with the focus on the toy stove and sinks in the far corner of the 20 by 20 room. There are four-foot tall shelves with toys grouped roughly in categories. All of the weapons are on one shelf, the rubber dart guns, plastic swords, shields, clicking cap guns. The stove has plastic plates, plastic food, utensils, and a plastic phone. "Who is calling you?" he always asks, "who do you want to call? Do you want mommy on drugs? Daddy gone? Molesting step dada, abuser cousins? Neglectors and abandoners? A cast of perverts, druggies, petty criminals, felons, irresponsible and selfish caretakers, people who had no right to have children?

Carrie's mom is a passably pretty 20-year-old who's had four men in her life during Carrie's short stint on this earth. Mom seems innocent, but once her husband had married her, she treated him like a parent and got curious about other men, living out that adolescence she never had. Dad is a huge, wide-shouldered Pole who had broken Carrie's little arm in an anger fit. She could say things to him, such as, "You're not my boss," and put him into a sputtering rage.

He took Carrie's little cold hand and began walking towards the play room. Carrie spoke like a blonde, four-year-old version of Lily Tomlin sitting in the huge rocking chair. All of her sounds are filtered by blocked sinus passages. Once inside she goes to the four-foot Punching Bag man, who stands next to the shelf in the far corner. She hits it with the fury of a Tyson, and as it tilts, throws herself on it. Her own fury surprises her as the bag smacks on the linoleum floor, and she falls off sideways. She gets up and moves to the sand tray next to the toy stove. The tray is filled with toy soldiers, Indians, dinosaurs, and plastic foliage. Shelves nearby hold plastic baskets, trucks, dolls, a small old doll house, puppets, a puppet stage with a curtain, and a toy carpenter's workbench with hammers and saws. In one corner by the counselor's chair rests the tall easel on which sit round plastic containers of red, blue, green, and yellow watercolor paint. This was the room in which he did play therapy.

Glenn presses his chest against the rolling office chair turned backwards in the corner of the play room. The little blonde girl starts in one corner of the sand tray, and begins to put it in order, lining up all of the objects. Afterwards, she begins to put the stove in order. She knows what everything is, where it goes, and how it's supposed to work. Many of the toys don't work anymore because they're the objects of rage of hundreds of kids before her.

"It looks like you feel you need to clean up the room," Glenn says in the non-directive way they taught him to do in the seminar.

"That's what mommies do," Carrie says.

Carrie goes to the toy stove which has a little sink in which rests a plunger, and Carrie pumps water from the well into the tiny teacup she holds. "My daddy peed on me," she says offhandedly, "and he put some of it in me." Glenn switches on the video tape by the remote switch on the desk behind him.

"When?" he asks.

"Last summer when Wealth and Helfare made me go visit him. He put me on his lap naked and then he peed on me. There isn't any moa water. Let's get some from the sink." Now he understood her fixation with water all these months. They fill the plastic container in the stove. She pours it from teapot to cup, from cup to sandbox, from sandbox to the teapot and back again, trying to understand why the water reminds her of her daddy's abuse. She laughs a kind of crazy laughter, movie-style, a loony bin chortle.

"Daddy got mad at mommy for staying up too late, ad' they 'ad a fight."

"Which daddy?" he asked.

"Daddy Sean," she said. Before the separation from her stepdad, she had stopped pulling the baby around the house by the feet. She had started obeying her mom and step dad, going to her room for timeouts, listening at preschool. He doesn't always know why the play room works, but in her case she had felt some safety there and stopped acting like her violent dads. Now, it's mom's turn to act out.

Carrie pours the water over the Play Dough into the sand tray and then takes the Legos out and spreads them all through the gooey mess. She has done it while he daydreamed, and he has to say the rules again. It all has to be thrown away. "Did you know daddies are supposed to teach their little girls about how to have sex?"

Glenn finds it hard to believe what he's hearing.

"My daddy," Carrie says.

"Which daddy? Step daddy or real daddy?"

"My real daddy."

Glenn got the children's book from his desk, the one that talked about good touches and bad touches. He read it to her what it said about private parts being her business alone. "Daddy's don't teach little girls about sex," he said, "daddies are supposed to let you grow up safely." When he had finished the book, her time was up. "Mary…you have five minutes left. I'm glad you told me about your daddy. You won't have to visit him any more."

Mary gave him the look, meaning she wouldn't move. She didn't want to leave. When she lay down on the play room floor, he took her arm gently and said, "I have other kids who need the playroom too, and you get to come next week." At the threshold of the play room door he let her down gently on the floor and called to mom to come receive her.

Carrie got up and reached for his hand. Was he the only man in her life that hadn't left, broken something or violated her boundaries? "I can't wait to see you next week, Carrie. Good job, you did a really good job in there." He took Carrie's hand and walked back to the mother in the waiting room.

The End

Creative Writing for Counselors and Their Clients - Steve Flick M.F.A., LCSW

MYOGRAPHY

Some clients need to tell their stories as they begin to deal with the issues in their lives, and they need more guidance as they try and write or dictate their histories, especially if they've never done any writing before. I find the biggest problem is that new writers have trouble being specific. To aid in this process is a list of oral history questions, compiled from a variety of sources by Joanne Todd Rabun in 1993, presented in www.scrapbooking.com. While they don't have a psychological focus per se, many of these questions will lead to honest responses to issues clients have with their families, friends and culture (Idaho Senior News). Collect the answers to the following questions on tape or in writing; then, remove the questions and present the answers in toto. Also, allow for tangents, digressions, and all other material, which unfolds the story of that person's life.

1. Did you have a nickname as you were growing up?_____
_____

2. Have you had other nicknames as an adult? Do you remember hearing your grandparents describe their lives? What did they say?_____
_____

3. Do you remember your great-grandparents? What do you know about them?_____
_____

4. Who was the oldest person you can remember in your family as a child? What do you remember about him or her?_____
_____

5. Do you remember your family discussing world events and politics? Where were you when a particular event occurred, such as the day Kennedy was shot?   _____
_____

6. Was there a chore you really hated as a child?_____
_____

7. What have been the most important inventions during your lifetime?_____
_____

8. How is the world different from what it was like when you were a child?_____
_____

9. What kind of books did you like when you were a child?_____
_____

10. Do you remember a favorite nursery rhyme or bedtime story? What was it?_____
_____

11. Do you remember not having enough food to eat because times were hard for your family?_____
_____

12. What were your favorite toys and what were they like?_____
_____

13. What were your favorite childhood games?_____

Creative Writing for Counselors and Their Clients - Steve Flick M.F.A., LCSW

14. What were your schools like?

15. How did you get to school?

16. What was your favorite subject in school and why?

17. What was your least favorite subject in school and why?

18. Who was your favorite teacher and why were they special?

19. How do your classmates from school remember you best?

20. What school activities and sports did you participate in?

21. Did you and your friends have a special hang-out where you liked to spend time?

22. Were you ever given any special awards for your studies or school activities?

23. How many years of education have you completed?

24. Do you have a college degree? What was your field of study?

25. How were your grades?

26. How old were you when you started dating?

27. Do you remember your first date? Describe the experience fully.

28. Name a good friend that you have known for the longest period of time? Where did you meet, what have you done together, and where are they now?

29. Has there ever been anyone that you consider to be your kindred spirit or soul mate?_____
_____

30. How did you meet the person that you would later marry or live with? Describe them._____
_____

31. Do you remember where you went on the first date?_____
_____

32. Describe the circumstances where you proposed, if that person became your spouse._____
_____

33. Describe your wedding ceremony. Who was there?_____
_____

34. Did you have a honeymoon? Where did you go?_____
_____

35. How would you describe your spouse? What do you admire most about him or her?_____
_____

36. How long have you (or were you) been married?_____
_____

37. What advice would you give to a grandchild on his or her wedding day?_____
_____

38. How did you find out that you were going to be a parent for the first time?_____
_____

39. How many children did you have, what are their names, where were they born and describe what happened during their deliveries. _____
_____

40. Do you remember anything that your children did when they were small that really amazed you?_____
_____

41. Describe all of the cities you lived in and the houses your family lived in during those times._____
_____

42. What was the funniest thing you can remember that one of your children said or did?_____
_____

43. If you had it to do all over again, would you change the way you raised your family? How?_____
_____

44. What did you find most difficult about raising children?_____
_____

45. What did you find most rewarding about being a parent?_____
_____

46. Did you spoil any of your children? How?_____
_____

47. Were you a strict or lenient parent?_____
_____

48. Did you find that you had to treat each of your children differently? If so, why?_____
_____

49. How did you first hear that you were a grandparent and how did you feel about it?_____
_____

50. What advice do you have for your children and grandchildren?_____
_____

51. As a child, what did you want to be when you grew up?_____
_____

52. What was your first job?_____
_____

53. What kinds of jobs have you had?_____
_____

54. Did you make enough money to live comfortably?_____
_____

55. Did you work require some education? What and where did you receive your training?___
_____

56. How old were you when you retired?_____
_____

57. What were the hardest choices you ever had to make? Do you feel as though you made the right choices?___
_____

58. Who was the person that had the most positive influence on your life? Who was the person and what was his or her effect on you?_____
_____

59. How would you describe yourself politically?_____
_____

60. Are you radical, reactionary, liberal, conservative, anarchist, capitalist, socialist, communist (want society to live in communes), fascist?   _____

61. What wars have been fought in your lifetime? What effect did they have on your life and times?

62. If you served in the military, when and where did you serve and what were your duties?

63. If you served in the military, were you ever injured in the line of duty?

64. What U.S. President have you admired the most and why?

65. What are the biggest problems that face our nation, and how do you think they could be solved?

66. Describe yourself physically. How did (does) your physical appearance affect the progress of your life?

67. Where have you lived as an adult? List the places and the years you lived there and the domiciles you lived in.

68. Why are you living where you are today?

69. Do you wish you lived somewhere else? Where would that be?

70. Describe your general health.

71. What major illnesses or health problems do you remember having?

72. Are any of your health problems that are considered hereditary? If so, what are they?

73. What do you do regularly for exercise? What did you do in the past?

74. Do you have any bad habits? What were (are) they and what effect did they have on your life?

75. Have you ever committed or been the victim of a crime? What happened? How did that influence the course of your life?

76. Have you ever been in a serious accident?

Creative Writing for Counselors and Their Clients - Steve Flick M.F.A., LCSW

77. Has anyone ever saved your life? Who did and what were the circumstances? _____

78. Have you ever been hospitalized? If so, what for? _____

79. Have you ever had surgery? What for? _____

80. If you could change something about yourself, what would it be? _____

81. Have you ever had a psychic, religious, out-of-body, or other super-natural experience? Have you ever experienced déjà vu? _____

82. Recount some important dreams you have had recently or in the past. _____

83. What church, if any, do you attend? _____

84. Describe your religious beliefs. _____

85. Do you believe in an after life? _____

86. What was the most stressful experience that you ever lived through? What helped you get through it? _____

87. What is the scariest experience that has ever happened to you? _____

88. What kinds of musical instrument(s) have you learned to play? Who are your favorite musicians and groups? _____

89. Would you consider yourself creative? _____

90. What is the most creative thing you've ever done? _____

91. What have you created that others have enjoyed? _____

Creative Writing for Counselors and Their Clients - Steve Flick M.F.A., LCSW

92. How would you describe your sense of humor? Dictate or write a favorite joke of yours. _____

93. What is the funniest practical joke you ever played on someone? _____

94. What activities have you enjoyed as an adult? _____

95. What are your hobbies, avocations and crafts? _____

96. What was your favorite thing to do away from work? _____

97. What is the most amazing thing that ever happened to you? _____

98. What is the most embarrassing thing that has ever happened to you? _____

99. Have you ever met any famous people? Describe the circumstances and what happened. _____

100. What groups and organizations have you belonged to? _____

101. Have you ever won any special awards or prizes as an adult? What for? _____

102. Describe a time and place when you remember feeling truly at peace and happy to be alive. _____

103. Where were you and what were you doing? Who were you with? _____

104. What is the longest trip that you have ever taken? Where did you go? _____

105. What was your favorite vacation? What made it special? _____

106. What pets have you had? _____

107. Do you have a story about a pet? Describe the animal and what happened. _____
_____

108. Is there anything you have always wanted to do, but haven't? _____
_____

109. Is there a gift or toy that you remember treasuring in your early life? What happened to it? _____
_____

110. Remember a quotation which you feel is profound, and offer it as a final word which you would like to see others follow. _____
_____

THE VICTIM STATEMENT: A STEP IN RECOVERING FROM TRAUMA

During the 80s there was a powerful movement regarding victim's rights throughout the criminal justice system. Mothers Against Drunk Driving organizations were a part of that, and victims of homicide and abuse had victim/witness coordinators assigned to them to inform them of the progress of the case, the whereabouts of the accused perpetrator, and money was set aside to help victims recover from the effects of the crime, including therapy, medications, classes and legal assistance.

During the past 20 years victims have been able to read their statements, regarding the effect on themselves and their families of the perpetrator's crimes. In therapy the victim statement is a crucial part of treatment since it impels the client to articulate the psychological effect of boundary violations caused by the crime. It also has helped families forgive their victimizers in some cases. It has become a part of the therapeutic process itself, and many clients who have not pressed charges or have waited too long to go to court, are left without a public forum for their grief and loss except for group therapy.

In this particular case the mother, B.'s first husband, the father of her three daughters, died in his late 40s of a heart condition. Several years later, mom married a Hispanic man named I. He had played the role of the good step dad during their courtship and was able to persuade everyone that he was a kind-hearted role model. Religion was part of this façade as well. He started taking B. and the girls to church on Sunday. He constantly "quoted things from the Bible, yet he failed to live by what he preached." He began isolating the family from the outside, insisting that the girls be home from school thirty minutes after school let out. He disciplined the girls by making them stand naked before he spanked them for infractions, and at that point he began having sex with the youngest daughter, C. He told the girls that if they ever told their mom, he would deny it and punish them even worse ways if he found out. At first, C. did try and tell her mother, but I. Insisted it was just because he had assumed the disciplinarian role with them. Part of mom's therapy was centered on her not listening to C. when she first tried to tell her. The step dad would molest C. at night when she slept in her bed in her own room. He forced her to have sex when the family went on vacation to see relatives. Finally, C. told one of her friends at school, and the friend told a school counselor who reported to Health and Welfare.

I participated in part of the court proceedings when step dad asked to see his son, and the defense asked me to testify concerning the appropriateness of this visitation. I told them that step dad had lost the right to visitation, because he had also physically abused the other two daughters and his son during the years he and B. had been married. I insisted he go through twelve months of anger management and sex abuse treatment before such a thing would even be possible.

During therapy with the four children, each one wrote a victim statement expressing their feelings toward this twisted step dad.

VICTIM STATEMENT THOUGHTS FOR B.,

The mother (used with permission).

…Issues of control, relating to the kids and myself. The isolation of friends and family. The fact that he did not only fool me, but also my family and all my closest friends. The lies he constantly told me. It makes me wonder if our relationship and marriage was even real or if it truly meant anything to him. Maybe he was with me for one reason only, not love for me, but to satisfy his needs with my daughter. What a sick person. Lies he told others outside the family. He told people we were married when we were not. He told people my daughters were his when they were not. He put a façade around everybody. I hated the way he treated his mother. He would argue with her constantly. She too, could not reason with him at all.

Religion was very important in his life. He felt it was necessary to raise a family with strong religious values. He was constantly quoting things from the *Bible*, yet he failed to live by what he preached.

He argued constantly. His philosophy was that he was right, and everybody else was wrong. You could not try to explain things or teach new things to him. He felt that his way of dealing with the kids was the only way.

Other thoughts: How could a person that I loved and trusted do such terrible things to another person that I love and means the world to me? It seems impossible to me, but the truth remains that there are strange, sick people in this world. Like my boy says, he betrayed all of us. This is something that I will have to live with and deal with the rest of my life. I hate it that I am so trusting and believe that there is good in everybody. Thanks to this man, I can no longer trust people. That makes me feel guilty. My parents did not raise us kids with that kind of attitude. Unfortunately, the world has changed, so that people can't even be decent any more. What a disappointment. Thanks to this man, I will have a very difficult time trusting any men whatsoever. I think it will be difficult for me to ever have feelings for another man. How can I trust men after what he has done to me? I know that all men are not like that…It blows my mind that my own daughters are trying to tell me to start dating already. I think I need to set my priorities straight in life. As far as I am concerned, my kids will always come first…Thanks to him, the kids and I are at ground zero with each other. The fact that we can talk about all of this now is wonderful. I think we have all learned a lot from each other. I think the kids have a better understanding of what I was going through and what I felt, and what I knew or didn't know.

I love talking to my kids. They are funny, witty, encouraging, and so full of life. I hate that things can't be like when I was their age. There was much less worry in life. I cry right along with them in their disappointments even though they don't know it. I must remain strong for them at all times. If I fall apart, what then? I am all they have now.

I hate what he has done to the relationship between my children and me. I hate him for that! I am left cleaning up his mess. I have to be the one to try to explain to my daughter, "Why me?" It is not an easy task. There is no real good answer for that one. Of course it has nothing to do with her. I think K knows this fact. I just wish I could take away all the hurt, anger, frustration, fear, anxiety and humiliation away from her. I wish I could just hold her and say that everything will be all right. That is impossible because I can't say that with absolute certainty. That is what scares me most.

I hate that he has turned my daughters against each other. They have a very difficult time dealing with each other and trusting each other. Sisters are a special thing, and he has ruined that for them. I think deep down their thought is, "Where was my sister when I needed her?" I know about sisters. I have had my ups and downs with mine, but look who was right by my side through this whole ordeal? I guest I just hate life all together at some points. If I let that get to me, he will have won

again. I will not let him win this argument. I finally will have the last word. I just hope that last word is truly heard and does not fall on deaf ears.

I love the fact that I have a wonderful son. He is my son and will never have a dad. Suits me fine. Who would want a dad like him? He is the only good thing to come of our relationship. I really don't think he had much to do with it. Not to sound religious or anything, but I deserved a son. He is completely unworthy to have a son let alone be a father. He may talk about family values and what not, but he needs to learn to live by what he preaches.

I hate that I sometimes still think like he does. It took a while to go to the store and buy "normal" foods. Foods that were not sugar free. He is diabetic, not us. I have to find my own identity again. I lost it over the past five years. I have forgotten who I am. I need to quit thinking like he did. That is kind of scary. I have to be aware of what I'm thinking and is it me or him?

I hate the fact that he put our lives on hold for so long. He has forced us to leave our home and our lives. I have had to change all of our habits so nothing is like it was. I have a son who is afraid of a daycare because that is where the police came and took him away from me. I have a daughter that can't go back to school without other kids looking at her and talking behind her back. Kids are mean and they call her names. Boy, that helps the healing process now, doesn't it?

I JUST PLAIN HATE, HATE, HATE, HATE, HATE, HATE HIM!!!!!!!!!!!!!!!!!!

I hope that his punishment fits the punishment and torment he put my daughter through. Nothing would make me happier at this point than that. I just hope the judicial system works in your favor. He is very manipulative and sneaky. He has fooled many people throughout his life. My friends and family accepted him. They too are feeling a little foolish and betrayed. I praise my daughter for her bravery to see that others know about this man.

VICTIM STATEMENT, K., 13

Feelings: Fear, anger, hurt, embarrassed, humiliation, intimidation, threatened, controlling.

Why? I feared him because when he spanked me, he would yell and shout and tell me not to cry, and he would have a big metal ruler or a wooden stick. I was angry with him because he manipulated my family members. He always lied to my mom when he would punish us. He would tell me that he told my mom, and he never did, not once. He hurt me very badly by telling me never to talk about my dad. He recorded over all of our home videos with my dad in them. We searched everywhere for videos; we asked the_____ and the _____ families. We looked at the end of every video we owned to see if there was anything left of my dad at the end. We couldn't find one of them.

He made me embarrassed because the people who knew about what was happening would tease me. I was also embarrassed because he would sometimes (once or twice) would make me take off all of my clothes to give me a spanking. He humiliated me by just sitting there looking at me while I was standing there naked. He would always tell me that I was an airhead or a fat cow, and I needed to lose weight. I felt threatened by him because he would always tell me that he had cholos watching me everywhere I went. He always told me that if I told anybody, he would tan my hide. So, I was scared to tell anybody. He was controlling by not letting me play any sports. He hated soccer, softball, basketball, every sport possible except football. We would hardly have any friends over. He would get me in trouble if I got a "C" or below on my grades in school. I was scared to death to go home because I knew that if he was home after school. I would be in trouble for something. He said that if we had our nails painted, we would be a slut. He would always tell my brother to pinch my boobs. I feel like he needs to be locked up because he was teaching my little brother to be just like him.

FEAR: I fear him now because he is looking at life in prison, so I'm scared that he will come and break into the house and abuse and kill me or hurt me badly because it won't matter to him if he kills us because he will already have life in prison, so he won't care. I am angry still because he has hurt my family so bad. We live in fear now.

I am also still hurt because I want the videos back that he recorded over. I am still embarrassed when people find out because I feel dumb for not telling anybody.

Here's an example of a creative solution to the issues caused by sexual abuse within a family and a writing exercise to help unfurl the specifics of abuse. As this case unfolded, it revealed itself to me as an almost "tribal" solution to the stigma carried by the abuse perpetrated by a stepdad upon the youngest daughter in a family of three young women. Sarah (a pseudonym) was thirteen at the time the abuse began by stepdad. Mom had remarried after her first husband had died at a young age. The other two daughters were two and three years older than Sarah. Stepdad came into the family and immediately began to physically and mentally control the family. For example, he found every videotape of mom's former husband, and recorded over them, so that by the time his trial began, there wasn't a trace of the "good" father around.

Step dad was Hispanic and himself the product of a sexually abusive father. He would ground Sarah who had to remain home with him while mom and the other daughters went places. He told Sarah that he would kill her if she told. He molested her on vacations in strange places, such as closets, bathrooms and garages. He made her perform oral and anal intercourse and degraded her and her sisters by making them stand naked as he punished them for trumped-up offenses.

The girls had tried to tell their mother, but it was so unbelievable, it took her a long time to believe them. Eventually, they told someone at school, who called Health and Welfare. An investigation ensued and stepdad was arrested, tried, convicted and sent to prison for twenty years.

Meanwhile, the family began treatment as a result of this traumatic experience. Sarah developed symptoms of severe PTSD, including triggers (she couldn't sleep in her own bed), behavior problems, nightmares, oppositional acting out, and rages at her mother for not believing her. Her sisters, while their experience was not directly sexual, nonetheless had been controlled and humiliated by step dad with the restriction of their movements around town and being spanked while nude. The girls began hanging out with boys at the park. It always seemed as if Sarah were the one who received all of the sexual advances and innuendoes. Many of these boys were Hispanic as well. Two years after working with this family, mom called me to have an all morning session with the girls because they had made a pact to have sex with random partners because that way Sarah wouldn't be the only one who had been stigmatized.

I was stunned by the simplicity, the comradery, and the therapeutic nature of their communal act. This is not, at first glance, a therapeutic response to their behavior. In a sense the two sisters had sacrificed their virginity and reduced the shame of Sarah by having sexual relations too! Nowhere in the therapy books have I ever seen a more effective behavior for breaking a "trauma bond" like this one. The girls were literally taking back control of their own bodies from the step dad, joining Sarah as sexually experienced young women, thereby reducing her shame suffered at step dad's hands.

To help them discuss the issues caused by early or premature sexual activity, I prepared a list of questions for them to work through in therapy with me that might help a girl or boy 12-15 talk about his or her feelings after a first sexual experience. Some of them are purposefully graphic since they might be the focus of the pubescent client struggling with the reality of early sexual experience.

YOUNG PEOPLE WRITING ABOUT THEIR FIRST SEXUAL EXPERIENCES

Answer the questions with a complete sentence.

Do you have fantasies that your sex partner will marry, live with, have children with you?

How do you feel physically and emotionally after sex?

In Idaho the age of consent is 16. If things get out of control in your house, there's a possibility Health and Welfare could say you might have to return to foster care.

Does this person listen to your feelings?

How has sex changed your relationship to friends and people in your family?

Did you use condoms?

Did the partner volunteer to provide the birth control?

If you are under 16 and your partner is over 18, he may be guilty of statutory rape.

What rules should still apply in your house at this point?

Does your mother feel that having sex is a sign that you are no longer a child?

How did your body respond when you had sex?

Can you talk to your partner after he has had an orgasm? And do you know what that is?

Do you have anything in common with your partner?

What new, adult emotions are you feeling or understanding now that you have had sex?

In what way is sex less of a big deal, and in what way is it more? _____
_____

Do you understand something about how/why sexual behavior is so important and powerful? _____
_____

Do you feel strong enough to know when you don't want sex, or that you can stop having sex for awhile if you want to? _____
_____

Have you had any physical changes since you had sex? _____
_____

Does having sex/making love mean you think you'll get married after high school and not go to college?
_____

Are you prepared to communicate with your sex partner your fears, needs, and worries? Will he/she listen?
_____

What does your partner think of you now socially after sex? Is he/she treating you the same or differently?
_____

Please read about Chlamydia, gonorrhea, syphilis, herpes and AIDS from Planned Parenthood, so that you do not ruin your sex life for good because you are ignorant of symptoms or how to get treatment.
_____

Describe your partner's behavior during sex. _____
_____

Do you want to spend time with him or her and grow closer? _____
_____

Did your partner want to have or do anything unusual during sex? _____
_____

What have you noticed or learned about yourself since having sexual relations? _____
_____

Were drugs and alcohol or coercion involved in any way? _____
_____

What questions do you have now about sex _____
_____

WRITING ABOUT RELATIONSHIPS, ASSESSING PERSONALITY, PRACTICING WITH FEELINGS, RELIVING FAMILY DRAMAS

I have worked with couples for nearly fifteen years, and during that time the predominant pattern has been that the female in the relationship knows there's a problem, and when she suggests counseling to her male partner, he refuses for various reasons, and attempts to make his partner feel "crazy" by saying he or she is the one with issues. During the past year I have been working with Phil Deluca's *Couple's Treatment with an Uncooperative Partner* in which he outlines a treatment plan for couples in which one partner refuses to work on issues. After an assessment, which consists of three circles by the client in treatment, and these circles indicate how much "I" from the client's perspective, how much "I" from the uncooperative partner's position, and how much "We" from the perspective of the marriage. This helps the therapist determine if his or her client is an "Emotional Pursuer" or an "Emotional Distancer." Pursuers overdose on "we-ness," and Distancers overdose on self-centeredness.

With this paradigm it is possible to help the client who has come to therapy to stop the pursuit, without the participation of the Distancer. I used to play a negative game in my relationships called "I'm Leaving, do you Love Me?" This is an original game which came out of my parents' struggle to reproduce their emotional and physical abandonment by temporarily abandoning the family themselves to see if anyone indeed did love them. Then they would come back to a tearful gathering of those who remained. My mother added two sub-scenes called "It's All Your Fault," and "Give this Goodbye Note to your Father for me." The power of this game haunted me until well into my late thirties until I began my own counseling in earnest with Counselor Kate in Hawaii. The idea was to encourage pursuit on the part of my partner or wife, and then feel wanted because they came after me.

According to Deluca, the basic intervention begins with stopping pursuit. This simply ends the game of the Distancer. In fact, I am now able to predict within a week or so, when the Distancer will realize he or she is no longer being pursued and will try to entice the Pursuer back into a relationship again. But first, there are "Four Stages of Resistance by the Distancer" (DeLuca, p. 40). Stage one: Nice – "bait and switch" stage.

Stage two: Ugly—accusations, lies, manipulation, he wants to talk and discuss certain issues, blame, divorce. Stage three: Threats—"If you don't stop this (put me at the center of your life again), it will be all over, and it will be your fault." Stage four: Change or Leave—which one he or she chooses depends on the amount of caring he or she has for the partner.

This particular book, by the way, is a good example of email/chat therapy done over the Internet. Deluca has catalogued his correspondence with counselors and seminar participants who have used this method in demystifying their relationships. The other aspect of Deluca's approach is that therapy does not necessarily require that clients delve into the psychoanalytic details of their pasts; it is very existential and brief.

This section I've decided to put into italics because it represents a somewhat cynical but realistic voice I sometimes use when I have seen too many men and women reveal illusions and delusions about love, such as this woman from a dating service. "I always believed that there is someone out there for everyone. But not until I subscribed to your dating service did I find my 'Soul mate.' We couldn't be more perfect for each other."

"The Primal definition of love is letting someone be what he or she is. This can only happen when needs are fulfilled… love involves feeling the self. It cannot be transferred to someone else…love is the search for what was missing in the family of origin or with early caretakers (Janov, p. 290)." A Pursuer will generally use the same terms of the subscriber to the dating service. There is someone "out there" called a "Soul mate" and we are "perfect" for each other. A Pursuer is someone who has a history of being deprived of love by one or the other or both parents or caretakers. This creates a Co-dependent dynamic between that Pursuer and anyone with whom there is a romantic relationship.

In the case of many men they do not marry the women to whom they are truly attracted to because they haven't resolved the issues with their mothers. Instead, they will marry someone who is cold and critical (the issues that their own mothers struggled with) in an attempt to try and change that partner into a warm and accepting person. The struggle is much more important than the attraction. That's why so many of our movies are confused and ambivalent when it comes to commitment and marriage. At the end of The Graduate Dustin Hoffman's character shows up at the altar to "rescue" the daughter of a woman with whom he has slept! There is a long pursuit scene in which he drives frantically up the coast to Berkeley where he tries to convince her he should be forgiven for sleeping with her mother. Hoffman's character has been pursued by the mother and for a while he finds this interesting, but then she becomes domineering and he has to leave her and endure the humiliation of having slept with her to pursue the girl of his dreams. The movie ends when they drive away, as they always do.

AFTER THE HAPPILY EVER AFTER

After the ceremony, then the work begins. The work involves being honest about all of the experiences and feelings which each partner has as they come up. If feelings aren't expressed, "garbage" starts to pile up on the marriage ship, and it begins to sink. The perfect Soul mate begins to look ugly when he or she starts piling up credit card debt, drinking or using drugs, abusing the spouse, having affairs, and acting out the unresolved issues from the family of origin. Instead of looking at this behavior as finding out who the person is we married, I hear wistful statements, such as "I wish we could go back to the way it was when we met," and couples actually try and recreate the beginning of the relationship, or they have a second honeymoon. In reality, they are just getting to know someone they never really knew after the honeymoon is over.

Finally, there will be an attempt to have children as a way of bonding the partners again, and usually this is unsuccessful as well. Children merely stress the already gaping lack of communication and the widening differences in the way partners want to live. Half of the marriages end in divorce and 44% of American children are living in single-parent homes because partners could not or would not work on the issues they have between them. Sixty percent of second marriages also fail.

I recently down-loaded 32 pages of questions from the eHarmony.com Website, and you can look at them as well. If I write about what really happened to my wife and me from the time we met, until now 23 years later, I think that might reveal the reasons why I believe the things I do about romantic love. Loretta and I had both been married before. We started telling the truth about ourselves the first week after we had slept together (She had had an abortion, I had a vasectomy). Ninety days later we were in therapy together when issues started to come up. I had expressed a desire for an exclusive relationship with her, but she had told me about sleeping with her ex-husband and about a wealthy man who was coming to Hawaii on a yacht to see her. I told her I felt that would hurt me and that I didn't want to be set up for that, so I suggested we break up. A month later, after thinking it over, she said she wanted the same thing with me.

From the beginning there were three elements to our life together: Chemistry, communication, and then trust. In the space below, write about these three factors in your last or most important romantic relationship.

_____
_____
_____
_____
_____
_____
_____
_____
_____
_____

PERSONAL CHARACTERISTICS INVENTORY FROM AN ONLINE MATCHMAKING WEBSITE

In the original you are asked to check one of seven boxes of the questionnaire, and the responses range from "not at all" to "very." In this exercise I am asking you or the client to do more…to write a sentence in response to the statement giving an example of what your answer means to you. This particular set of characteristics is concrete and down to earth. Mentally insert the word "do" in front of every statement, for example, (do) I enjoy acquiring possessions? Write a sentence with a specific example from your life. Share this with a client and see what happens.

I enjoy a good joke._____
_____

I enjoy acquiring possessions._____
_____

I enjoy work for work's sake._____
_____

I enjoy mingling with people on social occasions._____
_____

I like reading everything I can about a subject._____
_____

I am satisfied with my level of emotional development._____
_____

I like to spend my spare time being physically active._____
_____

I am able to express myself in unique ways (e.g., words, music, art)._____
_____

My personal religious beliefs are important to me._____
_____

Creative Writing for Counselors and Their Clients - Steve Flick M.F.A., LCSW

I have a high desire for sexual activity._____
_____

I like to play pranks on others._____
_____

I strive to advance in my career._____
_____

I take pleasure in knowing I have done a good job, whether or not others recognize it.____
_____

It is easy for me to engage in conversations with people I have just met._____

I tend to think "outside the box."_____
_____

I view myself as well adjusted._____
_____

I need to take time to veg out._____
_____

I am a good artist._____
_____

My faith affects my life._____
_____

I greatly appreciate the physical beauty of the opposite sex._____
_____

I often see humor in everyday life._____
_____

It is important for me to be viewed by others as a successful person._____
_____

I feel a bit guilty if I am not being productive._____
_____

Being in settings where I will meet new people is an important part of my life._____
_____

I ask questions in search of information._____

I think it is important to continually try to improve myself._____

I care a lot about the physical shape I am in._____

My mind does much better with facts and figures than with concepts._____
_____

On a deeper level, you can do a genograph (see that section in the book) which will externalize the similarities and differences between your families of origin. For example, Loretta and I discovered we both had a grandmother who was paranoid schizophrenic. Our mothers were raised in Catholic orphanages and as a result were both carried anxiety and insecurity all through their lives. They had to manipulate and be in control or they would experience a great deal of anxiety. Therefore, Loretta and I can't stand manipulative people, and we keep them out of our lives as much as possible, and this is a crucial part of our understanding each other.

Write about an issue on which you and your significant share a strong opinion. Do a genograph and see what similarities and difference you have in your families.

_____
_____
_____
_____
_____
_____
_____
_____
_____

DO A GENOGRAPH OF YOUR FAMILY USING THE DIAGRAM WHICH FOLLOWS:
Dad's ParentsMother's Parents

Father Mother
_____
_____
_____

You
_____
_____
_____

Siblings
_____
_____
_____

CREATIVE MENTAL HEALTH ASSESSMENTS

Once you and your clients or students have written about their parents, and a significant relationship they are in, it may be already obvious where the dysfunction comes from and where it is going. In a therapeutic setting, we already use the *DSM-IV-TR* as our main diagnostic tool, but I've found that every ten years or so, the labels become loaded, and clinicians or teachers become wary of labeling someone Bipolar, Oppositional, Conduct Disordered, and become reluctant to create expectations for someone down the line.

One of the more creative ways of assessing clients, students, or other individuals I have come across is found in Gary and Carol Hankins book *Prescription for Anger: Coping with Angry Feelings and Angry People*, 1993). In it they have developed simple charts which help counselors, teachers and others who work with the public translate *DSM-IV-TR* diagnoses into more common and less loaded language. The charts help identify one's own predominant personality type and provide a general indication of the personality type(s) of others. They also provide anger management strategies for each type and suggestions for decreasing the likelihood that other people will provoke your anger. I have developed writing prompts that help clients and students identify specific examples from their lives to clarify why anger was involved (Hankins, Hankins, p. 156).

The alternative terms are useful when viewing personality types as more "normal" and less as "disordered." In other words, the Hankins approach is less loaded than the *DSM-IV-TR* and may be used in public without repercussions or negative reactions.

PERSONALITY TYPES: WRITE WHICH ONES BEST DESCRIBE YOU

Actively Withdrawn

Ambivalent

Compulsive

Dependent

Dramatic

Egotistical

Mistrustful

Oppositional

Passively Withdrawn

Self-serving

Remember that each personality type is not mutually exclusive, and each type contains positive as well as challenging aspects. First of all, look for your own type(s) and identify them. Then, identify the type you have the most problems with. Identify your significant other and compare. You could even do each other's, and then share them.

Here are some assignments, which use the client's experience of drama to write out interactions between him or herself and his family members or other caretakers.

SCRIPTS OF MY LIFE
A script, according to Eric Berne (1973, p. 418) is "an ongoing program, developed in early childhood under parental influence, which directs the individual's behavior in the most important aspects of his or her life. It is an ongoing life plan which can be roughly categorized in three ways: Winning, Losing and At Leasting scripts. Eric Berne's inventive and playful use of fairy tales is significant because scripts are formed when children are most vulnerable to "directives" (do this) and "injunctions" (don't to this) from their caretakers. As a therapist when clients do these assignments it's important to notice the archetypes from which they draw their scripts, such as *The Lone Ranger, Rapunzel, Cinderella, Santa Claus, The Lottery, Rambo, Bird Cage*, etc.
Write a brief description of the house that your family lived in the longest. Imagine yourself during the most vulnerable period of your life or during the period where there was the most conflict in your family, such as a divorce. Reconstruct the dialog, behavior, and emotions of that scene.

___

Imagine that your family was hired to be the actors on a popular soap opera, such as *As the World Turns*. Write several pages of dialog as your family handled or didn't deal with a crisis in your life, such as getting pregnant.

___

You are a script writer for a situation comedy called The _____'s (insert your family's last name in the blank). Recreate the setting, dialog, behavior, and show how your family dealt with a common sitcom conflict, such as what to do with your aging grandparents.

Take out an old scrapbook with photographs of yourself as a child. Begin writing about the events shown in the pictures, and go into as much detail as you can remember. Document the people, places, events, and memories involved with each photograph, including who took the picture, and what happened before and after the picture was taken. This is especially valuable for those who cannot remember much about their childhoods.

Picture yourself watching the movie of your life in a darkened theater. Visualize an ongoing conflict or "issue" that shows you in the scene as you are experiencing it in real life. Then rewrite the scene showing it the way you wish it would turn out. An example could be derived from another picture. One which applies to my life is *Out of Africa* which depicted Meryl Streep's character as the Pursuer and Robert Redford's as the Distancer. I watched the movie with a young woman whom I was seeing in Hawaii, and when we walked out, she had identified herself as the Redford character, and me as the Streep character, and she said she wanted to end the relationship! The concepts of Pursuer and Distancer come from Phil Deluca's book *Couple's Treatment with an Uncooperative Partner*, 2003.

Another classic marital archetype can be see in the movie and TV series *The Odd Couple* in which Felix and Oscar typify the left-brained, right-brained polarity in which most married couples find themselves. Given that these are two men living together is important because couples are too quick to identify these traits as gender based, when in reality it's much more unrelated to gender than to particular families. In an unhealthy marriage, each partner is trying to force the opposite sex partner into fulfilling unmet needs from the family of origin. The woman may have chosen a workaholic partner to try and change into a loving, supportive and emotionally available spouse which her father couldn't be. When these issues are portrayed in the media, sometimes they are easier for clients to recognize than when they are ongoing problems in their own lives. I am remembering two movies about marriage: *War of the Roses* and *Fatal Attraction*. It is a therapist's job to identify any underlying psychiatric or personality disorders, or drug and alcohol issues which may be causing one or both partners grief in a relationship.

FINDING A THERAPIST, IF WRITING LEADS YOU TO KNOW THAT YOU OR YOUR CLIENTS NEED MORE HELP

Clients, students and practitioners who have not themselves been in counseling, may discover through writing in this book, that they have some deep-seated issues which need to be work on with a professional. Thirty million Americans will need some type of help from a mental health professional at some point during the life span. If that applies, learn more steps in this path from a professional counselor, therapist, psychiatrist, clinical social worker, or psychologist. If you are reading and writing in this book for the first time, get a friend to help refer you to a mental health professional. Here's how.

Creative writing can be effective, but it can also help to work with a therapist or counselor to better understand the context of the memories, emotions and thoughts which emerge during the writing. The next step could be to participate in the counseling experience. My main source for this is Su-Jin Yim's article entitled "How to Seek Help" (10/28/01 *Oregonian*), and fifteen years' experience in counseling. At the top of the therapy food chain is the Psychiatrist, an M.D. with a chosen specialty in psychiatry. They can prescribe meds, especially psychotropics. New in the field are Nurse Practitioners and Physician's Assistants with many of the same prescribing abilities. Recently in New Mexico, Ph.D. Psychologists have earned the legal right to prescribe psychotropics if they take a 400 hour course in addition to their other training.

The Psychologist is a Ph.D. (doctor of philosophy) which often signals a background in research, though they also treat clients. Psychologists also are trained to do psychological testing, for example the Minnesota Multiphasic Personality Inventory, which is a classic instrument for determining personality types.

The Clinical Social Worker (of which I am one) is a practitioner who deals with his or her clients within their cultures, and family histories. A social worker with a master's degree (M.S.W.) may also have a license from the state making him or her a licensed clinical social worker (LCSW). To be licensed, one must have a Master's in Social Work and have completed a supervised, two-year postgraduate certification period, during which is practiced clinical therapy or counseling.

Counselors complete a graduate degree in counseling, marriage and family therapy and undergo supervised experience treating clients. They generally have a master's degree in counseling, or master's in education (M.Ed.) plus additional hours of supervision before they can practice independently.

Psychoanalysts receive several years of training at a psychoanalytic institute, at which time they take part in their own analysis with a certified psychoanalyst. This model is gradually disappearing from the scene because an analysis is so expensive and takes so much time.

Regardless of which background a counselor or therapist has, there are three major types of therapy, including psychodynamic, cognitive behavioral and family systems therapies. Psychodynamic refers to the approach that says an individual psyche is the result of family forces being played out in life beyond the family of origin. The therapist looks at how individual psyches behave in the family. It carries the advantage of having the therapist deal with the depth (psychoanalytical) and breadth (family systems) of their client's past experience.

Cognitive/behavioral counseling focuses on short-term problem solving in the present, with the theory that "our thoughts cause our feelings and behaviors, not external things, such as people, situations, events, and the family of origin" (Yim, 2001).

Family systems theory looks at the entire family as a complex system with its own language, roles, rules, beliefs, needs and patterns. This therapy can help clients "discover how their family operated, what their role was, and how it affects them currently" (Yim, 2001).

A creative therapist will find ways to use each type of therapy to work with individual clients. If I am working with a very left-brained client, I will have to refrain from exhibiting my spontaneous energy, going on tangents, and will need to take things in sequence. There are also some phobias and disorders which research has shown cognitive/behavior therapy to be more effective with, for example Obsessive Compulsive Disorders, Anxiety, Borderline Personality Disorder, and Agoraphobia. Criminals also do not benefit from feeling-process therapies, and instead most prison programs revolve around the "Thinking Errors" approach of Samenow.

So, now you want to find a therapist. First, you call up anyone who has been in counseling that you know, and you ask him or her who the therapist was, and ask how the experience was for this person you already know. This is probably the best way of all to begin counseling. Remember this: You're shopping…you're a consumer…you are going to trust this person with your feelings and they have to be able to hear you and go on the journey with you. For my money if the counselor isn't able to guide you toward your own feeling process, that counselor is not for you.

I have told my colleagues repeatedly that I am therapist in social worker's clothing. I began reading Freud, Jung, Adler, Karen Horney, and many others in the 60s, trying to understand myself. I worked in residential treatment of children and adult psychiatric facilities as well. I became "burnt out" and focused on my creative writing, attending the University of Montana's Creative Writing Program. I returned to counseling in Hawaii, working in the open and closed units of a psych facility there, but the most important part was my own work on my own life. My mentor and counselor Kate was the reason I wanted to be a therapist. My wife Loretta and I began therapy with Kate about three months after we began dating since there were so many issues going on around us. I recommend pre-marital counseling for every couple to help clarify communication and to eliminate repeating issues from other unions and from your original family.

During the first interview, find out if your therapist went through his or her own therapy! In Idaho I have found many practitioners who not had their own therapy, and I find this hard to believe. You don't know what it's like to ask for help from a professional if you've never done it. Furthermore, If someone hands you a *Bible, Book of Mormon* or a *Koran*, I would run like the wind out of the office because that person has an agenda and it's not your therapy.

I would be suspicious of a counselor who never recognized the need for therapy. They themselves have never been vulnerable enough to ask for help. The rest is up to you in deciding if the process is working. How does it feel? How do you feel? Of course, this is the central conundrum of human life. If I knew how I felt, I wouldn't be in this mess. The first creative step a therapist takes is to see if there is a psychiatric issue in his client. That is, is the dysfunction in the client's life so disruptive that he or she needs medication, hospitalization, and/or a DSM-V diagnosis?

Gather information, get a current book on psychiatric disorders, depression or personality problems and read it. See if you can find a "name" for what you are going through.

After clients have begun their own therapy, they will find the exercises in Creative Writing for Counselors much more valuable. The writing they do will document the psychic journey they have embarked on, and it becomes easier for them to put into practice techniques they have learned in counseling.

HAPPINESS

What is the payoff of all this work? I remember an earlier journal entry where I said "I just wasn't happy and I didn't know why." I've heard many clients, intellectuals, colleagues, friends and acquaintances say that it's not really possible to be "happy." Moreover, if you think such a condition exists, you're a fool for chasing it. *The Preamble to the Constitution of the United States* tells us we have the right to "Life, Liberty and the Pursuit of Happiness." Ah, there's the rub, the "pursuit" of happiness.

As I have come to experience happiness it seems to revolve more around being in the present moment more than having anything in particular. As I sit here typing this on the computer, I look at a list of thoughts I use with my clients to help them become more aware of their inner dialog. On one side are the negative cognitions. On the other are positive cognitions. Over the years I have let the paper of my journals soak up my thoughts and feelings through forty years of my life, and finally I know that I can feel happiness. That means I can be in the present moment a large percentage of the time.

I went to an eighth grade class at a middle school in Boise and taught some materials on poetry from Peter Elbow. I took my flute and tape-recorded music, and I discovered that after I gave instructions for a poetry game, if I turned on the music, they would be quiet and write, even though I was a total stranger to them. They all read several sentences from a free-writing exercise, and by the end of 45 minutes they had written at least a page of material, and some of them three pages. Then, they shared it with me, their teacher, and the class. This whole process makes me happy.

In relationships it's the same thing. Being happy with someone involves being in the present moment with them, not fantasizing on someone else, someone from the past, in the future. I am so thankful to my wife for being the woman for whom I gave up all my fantasies and for her wanting to be with me. I feel badly for people who were not able to find someone who would let them be themselves, and whom they could not let be themselves.

The article on happiness gave me some more interesting creative writing ideas which I will share with you here. Rate yourself on this happiness scale from one to ten for each item, one meaning totally disagree, ten meaning totally agree.

I am happy with my state of health_____

I define happiness as_____

I have more strengths than weaknesses_____

I compare myself with other people_____

I think people can change_____

I get over my bad feelings quickly_____

I have control over my life_____

I am productive_____

I love myself_____

I have all the money I need_____

My sexual/intimate life is wonderful_____

I like my looks_____

My spiritual side contributes to my happiness_____

My education was a great experience_____

My free/leisure time refreshes me_____

I have gotten the things I want in life_____

If I could live my life other I would change very little_____

I energetically pursue my goals_____

I can think of many ways to get out of a jam_____

My past experiences have prepared me well for my future_____

There are many ways around any problem_____

I've been pretty successful in life_____

I meet the goals that I set for myself_____

Arthur Stone's article in *Science* December 3rd, 2004, contains a "Day Reconstruction Method," during which you take a day and keep a journal of activities. At the end of the day, recall the events like scenes in a film. On average people report 14 episodes of varying lengths per day. For each episode, note what you were doing and whom you were with. Then rate how you felt about each episode using a scale of 0 for "not at all" to 6 for "very much" on each of the emotion adjectives below. Individuals will have to draw their own conclusions after rating their daily episodes. I think this is how it's done.

Rate each of the emotion adjectives below:

Impatient for it to end_____

Happy_____

Frustrated/annoyed_____

Depressed/blue_____

Competent/capable_____

Hassled/pushed around_____

Warm/friendly_____

Angry/hostile_____

Worried/anxious_____

Enjoying myself_____

Criticized/put down_____

Tired_____

EPISODE 1: I got up, showered and shaved, watched TV, packed, warmed up the van, and went to the Depot for breakfast. I talked with some farmers about a letter my boss sent to Boise from Buhl that took seven days. I was friendly, somewhat rushed, and anxious that I'd be late to work. Do some of your own episodes and see what you come up with. Numbers two, five, seven and ten are positive. The rest are negative. See which ones predominate.

_____

_____

_____

_____

_____

_____

JOIN A WRITING GROUP, TAKE A CLASS, ATTEND A WRITER'S GROUP AT BARNES AND NOBLE OR BORDERS, ATTEND A WRITER'S RETREAT

For the most part, all of the feedback one can get is valuable. Inability to receive feedback from anyone indicates a high degree of self sabotage. However, if the ego of the client is not very strong, harsh criticism can trigger certain clients into their rage, suicidal thoughts, rejection, and retaliation. This type of group is only for a seriously motivated writer who is ready to "go public" with his or her work. Some of these experiences are tough even for seasoned writers.

Currently, in Boise, there are two active groups that I belong to. One is the Boise Nonfiction Writer's Group which meets the first Wednesday of every month with a speaker who is a writer, an agent, or publisher who has words of wisdom and encouragement for the members. The BNWG also has a critique group which meets on the third Wednesday of the month, and during that group, members read their work out loud and get feedback, or they submit their drafts over the Internet, so they can be read in advance.

Another long-standing writing group is held at the Log Cabin Literary Center every second and fourth week of the month. An inspiring leader heads that one up, and twice a month, members show up to respond to the prompts he generates and then they read their responses aloud. Withdrawn writers do not have to read their works if they don't want to, and they can just sit and soak up some inspiration from the energy of the group.

As I write this section, one of my clients in a small, mental-health clinic in Boise, just got her book published by Lulu.com. Sara has a web site of her own, dealing with the occult and vampire lore, and she had her book on Lulu's website for some time before they just asked her to publish. She is receiving 20% royalties on her publication, and has an ISBN number. For Sara to receive this positive stroke is a wonderful lift to her self-esteem. She has had severe physical abuse in her childhood, and has turned her writing into a vehicle through which she is proving her father wrong. "He said I would never be anything, and I wanted to prove him wrong."

Sara's way of coping with feedback, critical or otherwise, is to protect herself by operating in the realms of the Internet. It's the perfect process by which she can cope with any depression which could come from negative criticism, bad reviews, and poor sales. The print on demand method does not demand any up-front investment, and there aren't stacks of unsold books sitting in the garage. She accomplished all this by being computer savvy and by keeping alive her dream on an ancient computer which she herself kept operating.

PARADOXICAL INTENTION OR INJUNCTION

According to McKay, Davis and Fanning in *Thoughts and Feelings: Cognitive-Behavioral Therapy*, 1981, Paradoxical intention is one of the fastest, most powerful and least understood methods of changing behavior. It is most effective in the brief treatment of individual symptoms that are perceived to be involuntary, such as insomnia, impatience, blushing, bedwetting, fainting spells, obsessions, compulsions, and numerous phobias (fears), including premature ejaculation.

One paradoxical intention I use frequently involves visualizing a switch on my or a client's chest, and the switch is labeled "off" in the down position, and "on" in the up position. When I choose to punish myself over being separated from my sons and being involved in two divorces, I first have to notice the inner dialog of punishment. Then I can say "off" if I want to shut it down or I can turn it "on" and allow myself five minutes to punish myself with the goodbye scene with Jake in the airport on the day I had to leave Hawaii to find employment. Certain scenes we replay encapsulate years of self-flagellation and depression and sometimes in therapy they can be ferreted out and replaced with realistic assessments of blame and victimization.

I have a client who obsesses over a battle with her narcissistic-borderline brother who is trying to steal the family fortune. She has learned to give herself the power to turn on the switch to obsess (that's called "prescribing the symptom") or turn it off; either way she assumes control over the switch (the cognitions, the thoughts), especially when they prevent her from sleeping. She first has to notice the obsessive thoughts. Then she has to decide if she will allow herself to obsess over the situation or to allow herself to stop.

The above authors note that many changes occur spontaneously. I still believe you have to prepare for the spontaneous change with therapy. Another example of a paradoxical intention comes from couples counseling. Occasionally, I will ask a couple who is having trouble making love to each other to not have sex. I am prescribing the symptom they already have, namely they can't approach each other to be intimate. I am expecting them to rebel, hoping that they will not be such "good boys and girls" that they will rebel against my injunction. "Who is he to tell us what to do?"

Some more examples of paradoxical injunction

include telling insomniacs to stay up all night, ordering perfectionists to make mistakes. Sometimes we just have to be tricked into making a change by taking the pressure off the direct assault on the symptom. "Bobby I want you go to home and pick three verbal fights this week with your sister and tell her that you're doing it deliberately." Reframing is the behavioral therapist's mode of getting the client to look at the world in a different light. When you are hiding your nervousness from your audience, you are lying to them, is one such example of reframing.

Have your students or clients write a problem here. Then devise a paradoxical injunction for it. Reframe your problem in your own language. Being nervous is a sign that you care about your presentation.

_____
_____
_____
_____
_____
_____
_____
_____
_____
_____
_____
_____
_____
_____
_____
_____
_____
_____
_____
_____
_____
_____
_____
_____
_____
_____
_____
_____

THE CREATIVE PROCESS

Creativity in America is something that is admired in the abstract. I think this is because the artist in this country is only validated when he or she achieves notoriety or financial success. In the meantime, an artist or innovator of any type puts new information into the culture, and the audience waits to see if somebody else accepts the information.

Creativity in American culture is a two-way street because while appreciate and value the creativity of successful creators, we are not sure how to react to creative people in the process of finding a creative voice. The creator may upset some important people in business, education, medicine, art, government, or politics. Teachers have difficulty with creativity because they are in a social situation where it may be appreciated one minute and may be vilified the next, either because of content or style.

The minute a student literally and figuratively "colors outside the lines" the teacher is in a quandary. Does this student need to follow directions, or explore? Does the exploration lead to questions I can't answer, and does it mean I lose control of the classroom? Can I make a move without research backing me up? These are continual conundrums that counselors and teachers face, and each one of us has to make a decision concerning how to function within an educational and social system.

I solved the problem by working in the community college system in which all of the students were theoretically "adults" and where unusual teaching methods could be employed without political flack being directed at me. I shared and developed my own materials which I got to use in my own classrooms, making it much easier to get behind the relevance, interest and development of each student's writing ability. The problem is most textbooks are not written for students, they're written for publishers and colleagues.

One of the major works about creativity comes from Mihaly Csikszentmihalyi's (Sashentmihali) *Creativity: Flow and the Psychology of Discovery and Invention*. I have extracted 26 behaviors that will help you as a teacher or counselor enhance your creativity, and most of these come from his chapter 14 titled "Enhancing your Personal Creativity."

Not everyone can deal with the issues creativity creates in one's life, and there is profound sacrifice of time and money. To complete a poem, song, short story, novel, or piece of creative non-fiction still requires a vision of how the pieces of life fall or don't fall into an organic whole. One irreplaceable part of fiction and poetry writing involves narrative "voice" since the voice of the writer or the narrator in creative writing provides the invisible guiding hand which selects which is important and which is not. I envy the videographers, photographers, computer-generated artists, movie makers, and recording engineers who can escape the drudgery of describing the terrain in which their characters live, but I don't envy them when they fail to find any content for their media.

For clients as well, creative writing provides a way for them to express the desire for wholeness, which is lacking in their own lives, and in this way the client with a psychiatric disorder can sometimes reach out to an audience if she or he can find a "voice" for her experience through fiction.

Writing programs in prison, for example, have helped the most hopeless people in our society find a way to express their condition. In the sixties I remember reading Jean Genet's work that seemed to embrace degradation and portray it as a way of describing the experience of having nothing to lose, and then rising from that stance.

Creativity seems to be absent in most of our institutions. When you look at American institutions today, there is strong evidence that as much as they have a positive contribution to make, for many people they have become experiences which create stress and which create a need for survival skills. Reflect on your own experience of our hospitals, medical care system, education system, corporations, the military, higher education, the law enforcement and correctional systems, mental health, social security, our governmental agencies, and lastly the insurance and financial institutions, symbolized by Wall Street and the attending behaviors of the stock market. As individuals we have had to become our own doctors, teachers, corporations, law enforcement, prison guards, and financial managers.

A good way to run through this is to write a sentence or two responding to some or all of the suggestions. Do this by writing about any experience or lack of experience in the behaviors. Which ones are lacking in your personal creativity, and which ones are you already practicing? The best way to be a more creative teacher or counselor is to become more creative yourself.

The basic nature of creativity is making order out of chaos, even if the creator decides to express his or her creativity in a disorderly way! If the creative act becomes addictive, so be it, as long as everyone realizes it's only a phase. There were years where I practiced my saxophone, flute and keyboard six hours a day. Creativity then was also an escape for me from communicating my feelings to those around me, but eventually I learned how to integrate work, music, writing, and relationships in my life.

ENHANCING YOUR PERSONAL CREATIVITY

Learn your domain (where your passion is)._____

Get rid of the trash._____

Choose a discipline natural to you (my journal)._____

Embrace inner conflict (curriculum or freedom)._____

Pretend you're in jail._____

Enjoy your process for its own sake._____

Don't quit your day job! (Author's)._____

Find a mentor._____

Find out what your best rhythms are for sleeping, eating, relating, and working and abide by them, even when it is tempting to do otherwise._____

Explore the "shadow" side of your nature._____

Get in touch with your feelings and stay in touch._____

Frame this behavior in terms of your "gift" to the world (cognitive restructuring! Author).
_____

School can help and hinder creativity: take only what you need from school. (Author's)
_____

Tell the truth: our culture is full of lies about what's important._____

Learn to tolerate solitude._____

Stay away from negative people._____

Connect disparate domains (mine were English, psychology, music, sports, creative writing).
_____

Realize that each person has potentially the psychic energy to lead a creative life.
_____

Obstacles are internal._____

Develop a system to record what you see, hear, feel, touch, taste, think and intuit.
_____

Protect your creative energy._____

Turn off the TV (author's)._____

Take charge of your schedule. Declare bankruptcy; live simply, untangle your ego from the Corvette (author's)._____

Shape your space._____

Do the work._____

CREATIVE WRITING ABOUT MONEY

The only way to remain middle class right now is to create sheltered income for you. Maria Nemeth, Ph.D., has written an excellent book called *The Energy of Money*, and besides the obvious metaphor in the title, she writes this: "Money touches almost every aspect of living…everything we do and dream of is affected by our relationship with this powerful energy…this very discomfort is what makes our relationship with money such fertile ground" (Nemeth, p. 1).

Take out your wallet right now and empty it out in front of you. Empty your pockets as well. Hold onto a dollar or other bill and think about the people who have held this dollar bill and what they have used it for in the past, think about what you will use it for in your life, and think about the people in the future who will use it. In what sense do you feel that energy is money? Write about what else is in your wallet and how it reflects your identity. Include driver's license, picture, credit cards, membership cards, library card, student identification, etc.

Now, during the recession, millions of Americans are evaluating their relationships to spending, saving, investing, and consuming. We are being forced to examine how we have used or abused our precious life energy in pursuit of materialism. This next exercise should bring up some revealing thoughts and feelings about money.

WHAT'S IN YOUR WALLET OR PURSE? WHAT PARTS OF YOUR IDENTITY DO THESE ITEMS REPRESENT?

_____
_____
_____
_____
_____
_____

Eric Berne describes several great games which Americans play in regards to money. The first is called "Waiting for Santa" in which we spend our life waiting for someone to bring gifts. Within this game are "Lottery," "Talent Scout," "Inheritance," played by Trust Fund Bums, and "Pension." On the other side of WFS is "Waiting for the Undertaker." That is we spend our time waiting for death as the answer for solving problems for all losers. Illusions are the "if onlys" and "some days" upon which most people base their existence.

Describe how you play "Waiting for Santa?"

_____
_____
_____
_____
_____

Write a paragraph revealing your thoughts on what you would do if you won the lottery.

_____
_____

If you are creative, musical or artistic, write about your fantasy of being discovered by a talent scout or being discovered by "American Idol."

_____
_____
_____
_____

Is there someone in your family who could/might leave you money or property? What wishes or thoughts do you have about inheriting this windfall?

_____
_____
_____
_____

LETTER TO THE PROBLEM
This exercise uses writing to "reframe" or redefine an issue that a client is having currently. This one is tricky because there is a tendency to focus the problem or issue outside of oneself, instead of on the "I feel" aspect of the situation. For example, if a female client is writing a letter to her boyfriend who is cheating on her, the tendency would be to write him the letter. Instead, the client's job is to focus on the lack of self esteem which has caused the client to give away all of the power to her boyfriend.
This has been modified from Peter Elbow's *Writing with Power*, 1981.

1. What color is the problem?_____

2. What shape?_____

3. What is the mode of transportation of the problem?_____

4. Give a definition of the problem._____

5. Whine about the problem and blame everyone else you can think of. _____
_____

6. Imagine there was no word for the problem, i.e. Co-dependency._____

7. Make up a new one._____

8. Imagine_____is a place. Describe it. _____

9. What animal would make a good representation for _____? _____
_____

10. Design a logo or a flag for_____. _____
_____

11. What sounds, smells, tastes, touches, visual images are associated with_____?_____
_____

MORE

1. What do you get out of having this issue? What's the payoff? _____

2. The well's running dry. _____

3. A bribe will do the trick. _____

4. Bribe whom? With what? _____

5. God is angry. At whom? Why? _____

6. The problem has been stated wrong. Find three ways to say it differently.
_____

7. It looks like a problem, but really everything is fine if you only take the right point of view.
_____

8. There is no solution. What action follows this conclusion? _____

9. It's sabotage. _____

10. The problem was handed over to a consultant. What did she do with it? _____

11. You've decided to do nothing. What happens? _____

12. The problem reminds you of a situation in the past or something that happened to your best friend. How was it resolved? _____

13. Two kidnappers hold you at gunpoint and demand that the problem be resolved, or you will die. What steps do you take? _____

14. You are six months from dying from a terminal illness. How do you gain closure? _____

15. Make a collage representing your problem. Really, make a collage with pictures from magazines, scissors, glue, crayons, pencils, and write slogans that will help you come to grips with the issue. Put it up on the entrance to your house you use most of the time. Look at it every day. Then, do something.

THE CLASSROOM IS THE GARDEN OF DAYDREAMS (BEFORE 1970, ONLY 2% OF AMERICANS AGED 12 AND OLDER HAD TAKEN ANY ILLEGAL DRUGS)

THE CLASSROOM IS THE GARDEN OF ANXIETY (IN 2008, 45% OF AMERICANS AGED 12 AND OLDER HAVE USED ILLEGAL DRUGS.)

In the 1960s when I was in junior high and high school, the pressure on students of that era was minimal compared to what it is now. Also, if someone skipped class and was found by police, he or she was brought back to the school. Out of a class of 125, there were perhaps four or five students who were abusing alcohol in the whole class. Now, nearly half of all children 12 and above and adults are using illegal drugs.

Peer pressure, stress, and competition have created an environment in America whereby it's nearly impossible to avoid a period of one's life which does not include some form of substance abuse, hitting bottom, and recovery. The pressure of performance in sports, the arts, politics, and everyday life have spread stress throughout American Society. Many of the activities which we began in college are now experienced by students in junior high, namely sex, drugs, and rock and roll. Advertising and films have created the desire in our children to grow up quickly, and the result is that they have no childhoods left.

In modern schools, creative writing, and creativity in general are hit and miss experiences in the current climate of "No (special interest) left behind. The reactionaries (go to a past era or behavior) clamor for accountability via testing, the liberals (favoring progress and reform) get their children into charter schools, the conservatives (keep things the way they are now) use private schools and segregate their children from other classes, races and religions. There are now approximately one million children being home schooled in this country because the environment of our public schools is so unhealthy. Many home-schooled children are so taught because their parents want them indoctrinated into Christianity and use "faith-based" materials.

Then there are the Academies or Alternative Schools, which are the repositories for students with behavior problems, early pregnancy, psychiatric and behavioral issues, attention deficit problems, juvenile criminals, status offenses, such as smoking, drugs, runaways, etc. It's hard to describe the climate there. I visited Mountain Cove Academy in Boise, Idaho several years ago, and found that these students were alienated from a traditional classroom, or they were too distracted and disorganized to do much homework on their own.

The Academy atmosphere works on the basis of limited number of subjects per quarter; additionally, courses are broken down into worksheets, which must be done at school. And as a certain curriculum is completed page by page, the student is given credit for a class. The relationships are structured, behavioral expectations are enforced, and progress is focused on a day-by-day use of class time. The teachers facilitate the completion of the daily course work and are available to tutor and mentor students individually. It's hard to pinpoint the label for students, parents, teachers and administrators who are involved in alternative education. For now, I will call them Social Reformers (improving conduct and character, reshaping it).

The first sentence in my textbook for my School Social Work course reads like this: "The school in America is the mirror of society…however; history has taught us that the school as an organization is slow to respond to social influences" (Meares, Washington, Welch, 1996, p. 1).

Creative children and adults have a kind of "radar" which hurtles them ahead of others clustered around the norm. This doesn't hold in all areas of study, just in the areas they care about. As I review my school experiences, I had two excellent teachers from first to eighth grade, and I had two or three during my whole four years of high school. The rest of the seven or eight years was a waste of time. My seventh grade teacher understood that I was developing my radar when I began to write poetry and read Robert Blake. My buddy and I started our class newspaper. We made up satirical ads for deodorant and Pepsi. The rest was playground, sports, learning about puberty, and family life.

The classroom has not changed since the 14th Century, Marshall McLuhan writes in *Understanding Media*. He says the relationship between the electronic media, which are instantaneous, and the process of acquiring knowledge in textbooks, training teachers, with their propensity for print, has created a paradigm disjunction. Rita Dunn, profession at St. John's University, reports in her study that "70% of all people are not auditory in their learning style, and yet most of our teaching is done through talking, somewhat through writing on a black or white board. Very few people can remember three quarters of what they hear in a 45-minute class."

To use creative writing with a client or student, first find out what his or her learning style or blend of styles. Dunn has studied and has found five of these styles. Auditory learners remember what they hear. Visual learners remember what they read. Tactile learners need to get their hands on objects, models, and scales. Analytic learners are best learning in a sequence, step by step. Global learners need to see the big picture before the facts. Kinesthetic learners need to move, as they are being stimulated.

Are they predominately left-brained or right-brained? Have your clients analyze their styles by checking the characteristics which apply here.

Left Hemisphere	Right Hemisphere
Verba	lNonverbal, visual-spatial
Sequential	Simultaneous, spatial, analogic
Logical analytical	Gestalt, synthesizing
Rational	Intuitive
Western thought	Eastern Thought
Abstract	Concrete
Intellectual	Sensuous
Deductive	Imaginative
Realistic	Impulsive
Objective	Subjective
Material	Spiritual

These dichotomies are from Springer and Deutsch's *Left Brain, Right Brain*. As you can see creative writing is a strange combination of left- and right-brained functions. You must have the capacity to use images (pictures of the five senses in words) as well as having verbal skills residing in the left brain.

The modern student is prepared by television to have some sort of in-depth involvement with his or her education. TV and movies are "hot" media. They have changed the roles of teacher and student. The computer has also added to this change. Many times I have stood in front of my class, or have sat in one of the small group circles and have realized that many of the "students" have more expertise with the computer than I ever will have.

The computer whiz at 18 can embark on a career without any degree whatsoever because it does not take him any time to prove he has as much expertise as someone with a Ph.D. He can demonstrate it instantaneously. A teacher in the modern world is or will be more of a facilitator than someone who is expected to know everything. He or she will decide what media to use, what is relevant to include, how to organize presentations, which way to have students contribute to the class. The facilitator will choose and explore the relationships between books, tapes, video, DVD, movies, guest speakers, field trips, internships, as well as providing guidance to the students and using tests, writing, and oral presentations to get the necessary feedback for their grades.

Rita Dunn says that a healthy percentage of learning-disabled children are not at all learning-disabled, but they are "teaching disabled." The training of teachers has not changed much from the fifties to the present. There are still "lesson plans," objectives, students expected to sit in one place, and the teacher standing at the front, pouring knowledge into their heads, like water from a teapot. The teacher is competing with the electronic world of movies, computers and video games. The students require more and more stimulation because of their exposure outside of the print world of the school.

The fact is that as soon as the facilitator can individualize his approach to the students in his class, the more he or she will fulfill the need for "in-depth involvement" that McLuhan mentioned earlier. This is where counselors and therapists can be a tremendous help to teachers because they have the luxury of working one-on-one with children who are struggling in their public school classrooms. A therapist can spot a paradigm gap between the teacher and student and through written, phone, or face communication can diplomatically suggest creative ways to bridge the gap between a right-brained child and a left-brained teacher. After all, isn't that the source of most of the misunderstandings you experience yourself in this world?

Throw into that mix the environmental factors—such as whether the room's too cold, the chair's too hard, the light's too bright, the hour's too early, the activity's too structured, the group's too big, or the teacher's too autocratic—and you get a glimpse of the roadblocks to learning in a typical public school.

Then, there's the problem that information is changing at such a rapid pace, that by the time a textbook, dictionary or encyclopedia gets printed, it has whole sections which are out of date or irrelevant. The best examples are the breakup of the Soviet Union, all of the murder statistics collected before 1985 when crack cocaine became prominent in the U.S., and DNA research of the past five years. The whole machinery of printed textbooks is probably going to give way to computerized gathering of information and presentation in classes. In fact, one campus is already giving its students laptops which have all of their textbooks downloaded into them, rendering the printed textbook obsolete.

In all of these modes, the powers of writing, reading and interpreting, and speech are still the relevant real-world skills which students can take from an academic environment if they can survive the boredom. Ad executives still make presentations to their potential clients, trainers still get paid to introduce whole companies to new technology, medical sales people present complicated studies of drugs to physicians and psychiatrists, and the experience of putting ideas forth to a group is paramount. I have told my writing students that if they can read a teleprompter, they too can do the nightly news!

What is teaching now? I think it is the facilitation of information and the modeling of information to an audience which is counting on one to know something about the requirements of the job market. At least in college it is. There is the advantage of teaching writing because that brings with it a built-in skill. And creative writing has always had a place in the worlds of academia and The American Dream.

The Great American Novel is still a springboard for a writer's career and ultimately the sale of that book to the movies propels the writer into a socially mobile creator. What does that represent? It means that you have created something out of your own mind and experience, imagination and verbal skill which other people have bought, read, and hopefully admired. You have been loved and appreciated for verbalizing experience for millions of people. This is the ultimate "high" for any writer: acceptance.

The journey to acceptance is the story of all artists. It's based around the audience finding a writer who can articulate or render a vision which somehow clarifies for them what is important about that audience's world. Someone who comes to mind is John Irving's *The World According to Garp*. Garp is particularly important because not only does it render a world, but the story itself is a kind of writer's manual, a coming of age story which traces the character formation of a verbal artist from birth to death. It was the only book I ever read where I cried at the end when Garp is assassinated by the radical feminist in the gym where Garp learned to wrestle.

In Irving's book the world is envisioned as "an X-rated soap opera." That is, the pornographic is blended with the sentimentally and emotionally banal (insipid and pointless); thus, Garp's rival, the man with whom his wife is committing adultery, has his penis bitten off by her when Garp's Volvo rear-ends Michael Milton's car as the wife is giving him a blow job. The event is prepared for when chapters earlier, Irving has shown Garp performing a four-wheeled drift into his own driveway as yet more proof of his macho nature.

Creative writing, whether it be letter writing, poetry, journaling, Morning Pages, email, fiction, or creative non-fiction, song-writing, comedy, rap, or any other form, can send your students and clients on a life-time journey of discovery.

DESCRIBE YOUR SCHOOL EXPERIENCE
On the next page, go on a journey through your school experience, beginning with preschool, kindergarten, elementary school, middle school or junior high, and high school. Free associate on worst and favorite teachers, environments, classmates, and the content of your schooling. If you were to realistically design a school program, based on your experience alone, what would it look like? Now compare it to the way we speak and write about education in this country.

_____

_____

_____

_____

_____

_____

_____

WRITING ASSIGNMENTS FOR CLIENTS WITH ASSORTED ISSUES

The following writing "prompts" are not diagnosis specific. When clients do them for homework, have them bring them to the next session and read aloud with the therapist. The attitude/set of the therapist is simply to pay attention to which prompt the person chooses and triggers their positive energy as they write and share the assignment. The choice can help determine where the therapy can go next. Remember, that the client does not have to answer every question. The writing stimulates the memory and deepens the dialog between therapist and client.

THE "LEFT-BRAIN" APPROACH TO UNDERSTANDING A POEM

This approach comes from Aristotle's *Poetics* and from Karen Hess' *Appreciating Literature*. I have found students and clients to be thankful for some direction and guidance in writing about literature since to them it seems to be a secret language which only the instructor and a few experienced students may share. Using this format unlocks the metaphorical power of poetry for the young writer or client who is willing to use the layout. They deepen their understanding of poetry and increase their awareness of their own writing and reading.

1. Do a line-by-line paraphrase. Many students tell me they don't have a clue about their poem until they do the paraphrase. A paraphrase is a rewrite of the poem by looking up synonyms of the poet's key words in each line.

2. Write a summary of the poem; report the plot or story of the poem the way *TV Guide* describes a show.

3. Write a thesis paragraph which contains the primary assertions you wish to make in your analysis after you have done the other sections. This thesis comes about after going through the other steps. A thesis can be as simple as, "This poem derives its primary power from its use of images, diction (word choice), and allusions."

4. Write a paragraph which deals with the overall "structure" (hidden or overt shape) of the poem. Look at how it's divided into stanzas. Look at the poem as if it were a house. What shape does it have on the page? Are the lines long or short? How many stanzas or verses? What patterns do you notice are related to the content or thought patterns of the poet?

5. What is the poet's tone or attitude toward the subject of the poem?

6. Deal with the images the poet creates. Do not use the term "image" in its current vernacular. An image is a "picture in words of one of the five senses." Go through and mark which sense is being portrayed, and generalize about which is most important: Hearing, taste, touch, sight, or smell. This is the most important area of analysis in writing about poetry. It should take up more space than anything else. Write about the type and amount of images presented, and discuss the content of those images.

6. Look at the poet's diction (word choices). Look up all the words you don't know. Evaluate the poet's use of similes, metaphors, personification, rhyme, and meter (if any). Discuss alliteration, assonance, dissonance, connotation, denotation, line breaks, enjambment, caesura, and end stops. Look up all these words in a collegiate dictionary.

7. Write about the poet's use of symbols and allusions. Look up any references (allusions) to Biblical, historical, mythological, and literary figures or works.

8. Look up something about the poet's life and work. The *Dictionary of American Poets* tells you something about the life and work of most poets found in anthologies. Read also one short critical article about the poet which may help supplement your own understanding of the poet and the connection between the poet's life and work. Write those notes or quote directly, mentioning the critic's name and page numbers as well.

9. Now that you've done the "spadework," you are ready to write about the theme or main idea of the poem. Theme is what you believe the poet is saying in the poem. Theme is the total effect of the poem and its relationship to other ideas from philosophy, psychology, mythology, religion, and history. This should be based on your ideas arising out of the work from items one through nine. Also go back and write your thesis sentence about what the major strengths of the poem are and where it gets its power. A theme statement might start, "Rexroth's theme centers around the experience of someone turning forty and it displays the theme of reflection."

I developed this format and others in this book because I realized that instructors I had had in my own education had never provided the roadmap for me to follow. I had to stop pretending or assuming students knew things when they didn't and help them understand the concepts before expecting them to write about literature. Giving someone a roadmap is not the same as doing it for them. The road map gives students and clients the vehicles to do their own driving! Clinically, the format allows writers to see what can be done with powerful emotions to turn them into poems.

WRITING TO "VENT"

I first met LH at an assisted living facility where he began initially attending group on the periphery; that is, he didn't make a commitment to be in the group, he just hung around outside the group's outer edges. LH had been born in the same living facility when it had been the main hospital of a town of about 50,000 people. A doctor had previously diagnosed him with HIV and had given him six months to live. Three years later LH found his way to day treatment. Then and now he weighed about 105 pounds. In the past he had been an alcoholic/cocaine addict for over forty years. He had fiery red hair and a handlebar mustache. He had a very annoying personal style, consisting of angry outbursts as he responded to perceived injustices in the environment, such as, "Last week we got prize points for perfect attendance and this week we aren't."

LH had never seen a psychiatrist or a counselor, but when the staff abdicated the assisted living facility and began a new one after learning of Medicaid fraud by the owner, LH came with them to the new mental health center. During group and individual therapy LH processed his anger from childhood as well as his rage at having contracted the HIV virus from a female sex partner. LH and I deduced from his behavior that he had Generalized Anxiety Disorder and that he had been medicating himself from his early teens, and in fact was still drinking heavily the nights he was away from the day treatment center. Leonard had in the past been a supervisor in an offset print shop, and had wanted to be an English teacher in his youth. After he was unable to get a job in a local print shop when they found out about his HIV, LH took his energy and started a day treatment newspaper called "The Wild Bunch." The Wild Bunch News was edited by L. and can be found in the back of this book. LH has given me permission to use his story hoping to communicate to others the importance of getting to life before life gets to you.

This type of writing is called "venting" and its purpose is solely to free-write about any issues, which remain in the client's life regardless of how much therapy, medication or life experience he or she has had. Anything goes except homicidal and suicidal ideation—ask the client to save that for the session itself. Everything else is allowed to stay on the page between the client or student or counselor, and the reader should not overreact because the point of this exercise is to vent harmful thoughts and feelings without "acting them out."

LH'S VENT

I was just sitting around my place, in between household chores, bedroom, kitchen, living room, then the bathroom and myself of course. The stereo was on and this guy, no idea of who he was or what he was screaming about. He wanted to know who he was, what had happened to the person he had planned to become, what had he really become. There were many of him through his course of a life time. Each one wanting what he thought he wanted at that particular time and place. Things changing so fast, making it so very difficult to make the right choices. Never being able to go back and rectify, reform, remake, redo, reframe. Some choices are permanent, you mess up and it stays with you for eternity, no matter what. Those things build up, they start out the simplest of errors; then, those minor misjudgments pop up and rip the rug right out from under you without even the slightest hint, not even having anything to do with you of your self assured life of all that hard work that you and every other common man puts into his life for himself and family, not to mention that he was doing it for the benefit of his fellow man.

Blood was to have been the bond of family and when you come right down to it, the bond of a man on his word or that of a simple handshake. Contracts! Words on paper that anyone could make to mean whatever they wanted it to mean. Yes, I did say that if you worked for me, my company, for all those harsh and unforgiving years, those ungodly long hours, that I would make it well worth your while with promised of pensions, gold watch, health benefits, 401 K plans, social security, but that was 19 years ago we did not know the hazards of borrowing from Peter to pay Paul.

That, in the long haul, the bottom line reads "YOU'RE JUST SHIT OUT OF LUCK, YOU SHOULD HAVE BEEN SMART ENOUGH TO FIGURE THAT OUT FOR YOURSELF, AND NOT BELIEVED ANY OF THAT CRAP!! I SURE AS HELL DIDN'T WHEN I WAS TELLING YOU ALL THAT BULLSHIT ALL THOSE DECADES OF MY LIES AND DECEITFULNESS. SO HERE IS THE NOTHING THAT I SAID YOU WOULD GET. NOW GO WHEREVER IT IS THAT YOU GO WHEN I AM QUITE THROUGH AND FINISHED WITH YOU AND ALL OF YOURS.

Now here comes the part that I really can relate to and fully understand. It goes like this, give or take a few words. You need to go see a doctor. You have some real issues that I think you should see a professional about and DEAL with your failures. We know you have a few good years left in you and we feel that you are able to be retrained in another field that should just barely get you through the many long years of the rest of your miserable, worthless life. If you should be so lucky to live that long. See the cashier on your way out. Now that I have had time to VENT thank you for your time. I have to go home now to my place. I know that it doesn't quite shape up to your $250,000 expectations and lifestyle, but it is mine. I really wouldn't care if it was a cardboard box behind a dumpster. After all, I have been there. It didn't make much sense to me either, at the time, but when you have to go to the mission and tell the Brother Francis Monks that you had just stumbled across another homeless person that had passed away, due to hypothermia in the alley at the back door of the welfare office because they didn't allow it or they were busy with the lucky ones that had made it into the office before sign up time was over.

Those polite policeman were a good hour or so in getting to this very pressing incident. He slipped away quietly and unnoticed in my arms. I have to take that back. I noticed and if there is a God I am sure he was there to lessen his pain, it sure as hell compounded mine. I don't know that for sure as I still can't erase the memory of a friend of mine, let alone having to watch my mother for those three years suffer the agony of an evil cancer eating her up alive. What in the world was her children to do to defend themselves in this cruel world without her. Dad had passed five years earlier. Now what the hell were her children to do without parents to guide and keep them safe. I was a very young man in my early teens with two little brothers to look after, the other family members thought it would be better for them to put us into foster care or an institution. We were too young to know what was going on. We didn't know the actual meaning of death let alone know the feeling of not having parents or for that matter family. Yep! We would be better off that way because it wouldn't be their fault if anything good/bad should happen to us. It would not be their fault. Was this the way that things were supposed to be. Screw everything and everyone. I had no other way t o accept it. They were the adults. It didn't feel right by the way I was brought up by my father. I can't help but to have made a few bad choices in my life, but what would expect of me on my own trying to make all the right mistakes all by myself. No one else was there or even wanted to be. I went through a lot of self change growing up.

I used to look forward to school, to tell you the truth, not knowing what I would discover. It was wonderful. I wanted to know everything about everything and anything. It was awesome. My little brain was more than a sponge for knowledge, I wanted to be able to tell everybody. I knew that I had to be one of the most important people of the world, I wanted to be a teacher. It was easy to learn. I had good teachers, and I thought they were Gods in their own right. I did not know how they had become as smart as they were. I knew that my Dad and Mom were kind of smart but school was unbelievably overwhelming. I didn't want to go home from school. I threw a fit; I wanted to stay and learn more and if you I wanted to go home with the teacher, so she would be able to keep teaching me about everything. School was the only place I could learn anything, except farming and the like, and I don't know how they knew I was not even close to learning all that I was to know. I'm not even through learning as it is now.

I hate the waste of time in making my mistakes, but even though I put the major part of this, seemingly on some of the people around me, I can't stand to waste what precious little time that we all have to begin with. If you can't be a help to us all for us all I think that you are a useless waste of carbon. The sicknesses of the world are manifold and continue to grow. If God can see to let it be I think not. I know it as I live and breathe for myself. I can't see sometimes that it really isn't up to me by myself to fix the problems of the world, and that each and every one of us has a place for the others around us in our everyday lives. There is no greater Love except for the love of our creator, who ever and whatever we cherish him to be. He gave his only begotten son to us and he died for us in our sins so that we would never have to suffer that fate.

I am very disappointed that I was deprived of having a son, a child of my own blood, flesh, and body of my own. I have had the fortune of having a moment or two to raise a child of another, but it can't be like the real thing.

The future of all man is on the hair-breath brink of self destruction. Man has been a "Damn Piss Poor Care Taker of the Planet, the Garden of God's Eden." I am so angry at everything that I see and feel in the ways we mistreat each other, that what we despise in others is the ugly mirror image of our selves.

…I miss most of all the attitude that I had only to pick myself up and brush myself off and start over again. The stains are there. No matter what or when you try setting it right, the stains are an open book…I am in a rebuilding phase. I am not usually a religious person, it must be the season! The smallest infraction does not go unnoticed.

There is no way to take back a hurting, snide, rude and cruel statement…I can only apologize for my inconsiderate actions towards the rest of you (group) any time it happens. I am like Old Faithful. I don't know what I am up to right now, but at least I am alive…Why am I here doing this and not there doing that? I sure don't have any of those pretty wallpaper degrees, that we all want our kids to say, "Yes, I did graduate. I put a lot of personal time and effort to get it. I gave up a lot of fun stuff that I am sure my children will not understand till they have to give up one thing for another to have the best for them that is possible. Don't get me wrong, BAD CHOICES are a part of life. Some are life threatening, some right at the moment, others don't show up until years later often when it is too late to fix.

ANALYZE LH'S "VENTING"

Briefly, there are several images, which directly connect LH with his narrative vent. First, the homeless man who died in his arms emotionally foreshadows how LH believes he may die; alone in a back alley with some reluctant stranger holding him in his arms. The second concerns his bad choices which must refer to contracting AIDS from one of his girlfriends. There are references to "stains," his metaphor for how he feels about himself. Finally, there is the projecting outward the feeling that the world is coming to an end, which relates to LH's own urgency to make the best of the time he has left to live. LH experienced his abandonment through death when both of his parents died within five years of each other. He watched his mother die from cancer and there was no one left in his family who wanted to care for him; instead, they wanted to put him in a foster home.

This was the period when he began to drink.

Drug and alcohol counselors describe clients who began drinking early as basically remaining the chronological age as staying fixed because the person has developed no other tools by which to deal with emotions. Developmentally, the abuser cannot test reality, be in a relationship, respond to adult expectations, acquire verbal skills, communicate feelings, keep promises, and other behaviors associated with addiction. LH said that he could not go to work without drinking or using because he would be emotionally and verbally abusive to his co-workers. It took the reality of the HIV virus to force him to deal with a reality larger than his anxiety and abandonment

THE AUTHOR'S VENT:

(Diatribe: A bitter, abusive denunciation) It's hard to remember that one of the issues Freud was vilified for was to suggest that children are sexual. Because of my age I have seen several generations from the fifties through the millennium, attempting to come to grips with sexual behavior. Now, it seems in this generation it needs to be done all over again. One of every three females and one of six males will be in some ways molested or sexually abused between the ages of three and consent, which varies from state to state. One predator can molest hundreds of young children.

The reactionary (go back to an earlier time, denial of reality in favor of a public suppression of reality) atmosphere in our country is partially responsible for sexuality having to go underground, and to the dark side of the Internet. Religious fundamentalists believe that to talk about sex is to sanction it. That is why in repressive sub-cultures there is so much perversion around sexual issues. The human being comes into this world with his or her brain folded into two parts, and sexuality is built into the right-brained half of the personality. This translates into light/dark, selfish/selfless, love/hate, positive/negative, instinctual drives/religious prohibitions.

As I always say, "If you try and live in the light all the time, the dark side will get you from behind." The human being has a dark side; it's built in the "hard wiring," so you have to learn to journey through it and not make the detours. Many of the mysteries reside in the dark side, such as your sexual life, feelings, fears, asocial behaviors, creativity, dreams, the reason you were put on this earth, greed, generosity, death, art…these are a part of the human "script" as well. All religions have a dark side as well. Consider terrorism, the Crusades and the Spanish Inquisition, and also the Salem Witch Trials to mention a few.

In AA there is a motto: "You are only as sick as your worst secret." As the writer writes, he or she eventually is faced with the truth of his behavior, thoughts and feelings. As one writes, one eventually meets the truth somewhere in the writing. One day I saw that I was unable to say no to the women in my life. My own mother had been unable to tolerate my saying no to her, and so I had two marriages during which the time came when my wives wanted to get pregnant, but they knew I didn't want children, so they lied to me. I then had to face the issue that I didn't say no to them and mean it, and then later, I had an excuse to blame them when the children showed up.

When I finally took control of my reproduction behavior, I went to Kaiser Hospital in 1981 and had a vasectomy. The nurse was hilarious. As I think of that scene, I remember her jokes and diversionary conversation techniques to keep my mind from the operation. This is an issue that remains on the dark side of our culture, namely that many of us should never be parents, and that it's all right to make decisions to live consciously and without blame if you don't want to have children.

A LEFT-BRAINED WAY TO ANALYZE A SHORT STORY

Here are the concepts used in the analysis of a short story or novel. Plot: Summary in a paragraph, conflict, climax, coincidence, suspense, surprise, foreshadowing. Look up these words in a collegiate dictionary and write out their definitions.

Setting: physical setting or environment (time and place), social setting or milieu (social class of characters), identification of setting, significance of setting, setting shift, expectations of setting, overt or covert meanings of setting.

Character: Characters are the people in fiction as presented by the author. It is broken into makeup, motivation, moral values, conflicts and problems, character change, lifelike or real. Character is revealed in these ways: directly and indirectly. Does the character change within his or her possibilities? Is it motivated by circumstances? Does it occur within a believable length of time How does character reveal the themes of the author?

Style: The elements of style are point of view, language, atmosphere (mood and tone). Point of view tells us whose story it is. It refers to the eyes and mind through which actions are seen. Point of view is reflected also in whether the story is told in first person, second person, or third person points of view.

Language: There are eight aspects of this facet of style. Look up the definitions in a good dictionary and work from there. Diction, syntax, imagery, symbolism, irony, paradox, ambiguity, and allusions.

Atmosphere: this consists of mood and tone. Mood is the emotion called forth in the reader. Tone (of voice) is the author's attitude toward the subject and the reader. Adjectives which describe tone include objective, serious, humorous, sarcastic, tragic, etc.

Theme or Unifying Idea: This is the main idea concerning the comment made overtly or covertly by the author about the experience created in the literary work. My equation or shorthand for this is content=theme. What is contained in the story reveals its theme.

It's obvious to me as a therapist, teacher and writer, that the author's own inner dialog, perception of character and human behavior, and imprinting a theme upon his or her works involve highly sophisticated understanding of psychology. One aspect of fiction is to help a reader "see through" the iceberg to the unconscious basis of human life.

CREATIVE ACTIVITIES FOR KIDS TO WRITE ABOUT

1. Visit the humane society and look at the dogs and cats who are uncared for or abandoned and learn something about the child you are counseling. Read The *Encyclopedia of Dogs* and write about animals the child has had in his or her life.
2. Drive down the alley in back of the appliance store and find a box tall enough for the child to stand in to make a puppet theater. Ask him or her if she would like to color the "stage" with crayons or watercolors. Cut a hole in the box and develop a rudimentary skit which the child can perform for his parent. Visit the nearest thrift store and find used puppets, or get the cloth to make them.
3. Therapy is the remedial treatment of a physical or mental disorder; that is, to find a remedy. Play therapy is a way for a counselor to model for these parents who had no models for growing up. There is a whole generation for whom children are like pets who can survive on Spaghetti-Os, TV and a doghouse. They have no concept of stimulating and teaching their children to play, learn skills, have exposure to books, plays, music and sports. These activities help children realize their craving for an in-depth experience with their parents is not a hopeless wish. Have them write some ideas for their puppet show.
4. Go to the park, and on the way get a $.25 loaf of bread and let the client feed the ducks. Watch how the child behaves around animals. I tell them it's the "duck test." Sometimes the geese get aggressive and it lets me know how the child deals with the fears presented by these animals.
5. Buy a home schooling curriculum workbook of different grade levels, and ask the client to do a couple of pages to see what his skill levels are.
6. Ask the client to dictate a story and write it as they speak on the computer. Print it up and give her a copy to take home. The story may contain a paradigm of what is going on in her family life.
7. Use a Polaroid or digital camera to take pictures of the client. Tape the picture to a large sheet of paper and ask him how he feels about his hair, brow, nose, eyes, mouth, chin and the rest of his physical self. Ask what are his "favorite things" and understand something about the DVDs, subjects, friends, activities, food, teachers and friends of the child. Ask the client what he says to himself to get through tough times. You can do it? You're a big boy? Try your best? One family's therapy was a new motto every week on the refrigerator which the mother reminded simply reminded him to look at. The clients or students write slogans, mottos, words of positive regard for their looks.
8. A twelve-year-old pubescent girl who was an accident in the mother's life, is writing things she can do to help and make her mother happy around the house while her step brother is working his program in a treatment facility for adolescent sexual perpetrators. It's a chart of "chores" and "attitude." Others in the family can write acknowledgments of when they see her try.
9. Have every client under 13 draw a picture of his or her family members and include the house where they live. Have them write the names of them all and any pets they consider family members. It is not automatically known these days who is actually part of a family.
10. Spend part of a session helping a client with his or her homework to find out how she thinks. Type it on the computer and write at the bottom that your client has dictated the assignment to you, so the teacher will know.
11. Every time the parents come in ask them how the child did on the two or three behavioral issues that are being worked on. They can communicate this quickly by using a scale from one to ten.
12. Have the child write a letter to the parent who is absent, asking all the questions he might have. The therapist can assist with this. Many times even finding an address is hopeless, so the child can keep or burn the letter as a ritual of dealing with the rejection he feels.
13. Two children's books which have been invaluable to me are *Dinosaur's Divorce* and *The Touching Book* by Jan Hindman. Read these to every child going through a divorce or who has experienced sexual abuse.

14. Take a tough kid who is involved in the juvenile justice system and take a tour of a local prison or county jail. You don't have to say much. Have them write about the experience of touring the prison.
15. Cheyenne's mother came into the office and said, "My mother tried to spank her this week, and she said 'Steve said you can't spank me any more.'" I told her, "Well, at least she is remembering some things from her counseling." I had to coach this family to give up putting soap in her mouth as a punishment. Grandma used it. How did it work? Her daughter was a methamphetamine addict who was a prostitute until she went to jail. There was no awareness or insight around this fact on grandma's part. She was livid that a man had asked her to change her method of discipline.
16. Ask the parent to read the local newspaper's events section to find free activities for their children to attend. Most of the parents I deal with have no idea how to access Boy's and Girl's Club scholarships, library events, after school programs and community events for children.
17. Get a jump rope and take a hyperactive client outside to talk while the child jumps rope.
18. A 14-year-old Hispanic client is disrupting a family meeting by saying that when she's 16 she is going to get her driver's license and kill herself by crashing the car. Using Paradoxical Intention and/or Erickson's reality testing take the client to a funeral home and ask the client to choose a casket, pick a room, flowers, music and who would talk. It would also end the game to attend a funeral with this client and watch a grieving family react to their loved one's death. Have her make a list of choices she would like if she were to die.

FAMILY FEELING LOG

Here is a partial solution to the problem many families have: they have very little time to be together or communicate. Buy a bound journal for your family to leave on the kitchen table. In this journal everyone can write how his or her life is going on a daily basis. The first condition is that everyone must be old enough to write in the household! This also works well with blended families, roommates, unusual living situations, and groups where schedules preclude much face-to-face communication.

The log stays in the same place in the house and when anyone has an issue, he or she writes it in the log, flagging the entry with a brightly colored piece of construction paper. Members can also thank and show appreciation in the log. About once every two or three weeks the family needs to sit down and go over the entries, reading them out loud and clarifying the communication to see if things have been resolved.

LEARNING LOG

In home schooling, charter schools, private and tutoring environments, a Learning Log is a great way to document, respond and integrate all educational experiences into a single format. What really happens in a Learning Log is that the adults can see the inner dialog the student produces around the educational experience. Real questions arise as the log reveals the degree of understanding the student has about the concepts studied. The journal also helps integrate data, reading, field trips, lectures, and experiments through the filter of the individual student.

The simplest way is to have a 3-5" three-ringed binder, one which has a built-in hole punch. That way all brochures, writing, pamphlets and curriculum sheets can be placed in the order that the student experienced them. Typically, in the progressive school, subject areas are not usually divided into math class, science, social studies, language arts, and psychology. Rather, students go to a museum, read the local paper, watch a PBS Broadcast, get on the computer, work in a garden, and study environmental issues for science.

The log is the best way to help students focus on what they have learned during the course of a day or week. The learning is also personalized. Summerhill was an educational model from the sixties wherein students actually directed their own education, and Summerhill students seemed to pass the board tests when they graduated as well as students from more traditional public schools.

HELPING THE HELPERS

It's time in Creative Writing for Counselors for the teacher or counselor to do some creative writing for him or herself based around a concept presented in Donald Meichenbaum's great book PTSD: A Practical Handbook and *The Joy of Burnout*. I have a therapist friend in Utah who says that those who practice therapy or counseling have about 30,000 hours in which to do it. That's about 15 years of counseling at 40 hours a week.

In the case of teaching in the K-12 setting I know in my case as an Adjunct English Instructor at the 13 grade level, working with late teens, early adults and "non-traditional students" (those 30 and up), I noticed burnout after 14 years, and the last four were spent as a "freeway flyer" in the San Diego Area receiving no benefits, vacation, retirement, etc., and with all those papers to "grade" or respond to. Also, teachers now may work part-time jobs on the weekends or summers to keep their families afloat. It's all a part of the disappearing middle class which has transpired over the past thirty years.

This only increases our stress, depletes our Serotonin, and hastens burnout.

According to Dr. Dina Glouberman in *The Joy of Burnout*, p.2, burnout is "one of the words that seems to define this moment in history. No longer an unusual event, burnout has become part of a normal life cycle, along with midlife crisis, stress, and serious chronic illness, all of which have connections with burnout. It is…a growing emotional, mental, and/or physical exhaustion which isn't alleviated by sleeping; an increasing sense of being cut off from ourselves and other people; a decreasing ability to be effective at what we have always done, either at work or at home."

Glouberman goes on to say that burnout is what we do to avoid surrendering to changes we need to make. When our old ways have driven us to collapse, we can reconnect to our souls and our emerging truth. Burnout is pushing us to follow our love and our truth (p. 62).

Here are some indicators from Glouberman's book which can help you know if you or someone else are burning out or burnt out. Simply write yes, no, or maybe after each question, or free write an answer if you get some energy from the question.

Work is no longer a pleasure._____

Doing things for your partner or loved ones is no longer a pleasure._____
_____

You are doing more and more an accomplishing less and less._____
_____

You are doing more and more and feel appreciated less and less._____
_____

The list of tasks is endless, but you're the only one who can do them._____
_____

Your stress levels have hit the roof and are still rising._____
_____

It will all fall apart if you stop._____
_____

You are not doing as much as you should._____
_____

You are losing faith in yourself._____

Everyone else is talking or doing things too slowly._____
_____

You are in the wrong place doing the wrong thing._____
_____

You forget things easily or sit and stare in the air._____
_____

You don't quite know what you are doing it all for._____
_____

You are doing it all for someone else who should really do it themselves._____
_____

You are doing it all so that someone else will think well of you or at least not despise/hate/be angry at you. _____

Whatever you do makes no difference anyway. _____

You are tired of taking care of everything and everyone but can't stop. _____

You are exhausted all the time and sleep doesn't refresh you. _____

You have started getting illnesses when you used to be so healthy. _____

You are often angry, frustrated, cynical, and disillusioned. _____

You've stopped caring about your clients, colleagues, family or partner. _____

You are trapped. _____

You sigh or feel sad or cry for apparent reason. _____

You are detached from everything—no real feelings at all. _____

You have an empty feeling inside you. _____

You wake up and go to bed worrying. _____

You hate people you love, people who hate you, and you hate yourself. _____

You've stopped confiding in your friends and family. _____

You don't enjoy or have sex any more. _____

You are doing or taking in more of these: alcohol, cigarettes, watching TV, eating sweets, taking drugs, tranquilizers, casual sex, computer games, Internet chat rooms, trashy novels, living in your fantasy life. _____

You want to leave because there is too much to do. _____

The idea of getting ill makes you think longingly of crisp, white hospital beds. _____

The idea of dying makes you think you'll have some peace. _____

You don't remember why living is cracked up to be a good thing. _____

Working with clients or a high percentage of students who are in crisis can have a traumatizing impact on helpers and teachers. The emotional and personal demands, as well as the technical challenges of these professions can lead to "burnout," Meichenbaum writes (p. 278). It is also labeled "compassion fatigue" by Figley and "vicarious traumatizaton" by McCann and Pearlman.

Wilson and Lindy, 1994, have described two reactions to emotional strain experienced by teachers and therapists who work with traumatized clients. Under the heading of "counter transference," they describe two types of tendencies: Type I they characterize as the therapist's tendency to avoid and engage in empathetic withdrawal. Type II is the practitioner's tendency to over identify and engage in empathetic enmeshment (Meichenbaum, p. 278).

The most recent example we have is the 9/11/01 tragedy. Here are themes experienced by rescue workers who have shown symptoms of prolonged stress response.

1) The degree of force and destruction involved.
2) Confrontations with death (massive, gruesome and mutilating death).
3) Feelings of hopelessness.
4) Feelings of anger (that not more was done).
5) Significant loss and accompanying grief (identification sympathy).
6) Attachment and relationships that develop among rescue team members.
7) Elation of feelings of triumph among some rescue workers.
8) Survivor guilt (could not do more).
9) Voyeurism.

In order to cope with such distress, teachers and therapists need to engage in personal, professional, and organizational activities to cope with trauma and stress. Personal interventions include:

1) Recognizing emotional, cognitive and physical signs of incipient stress reactions in self and in colleagues (increased self-awareness).
2) Do not limit clinical practice or teaching to only PTSD clients; balance victim and non-victim case loads.
3) Limit overall case loads, hours of teaching, monitor case loads in terms of size and number of trauma cases.
4) Perform self-care behaviors, including "mental health days," relaxation activities (hot springs, massage), vacations, exercise, and therapy.
5) Recognize you're not alone in facing the stress of working with difficult clients and students.
6) Ensure physical and mental well being with good nutrition, sleep, relaxation, activity, creative expression, humor, replenish!
7) Use your philosophical, religious, and spiritual powers and visualize yourself as a "midwife" on the client or student's journey toward healing. Recognize limitations. Focus on the healthy parts of clients and students.
8) Share reactions with students and clients.
9) Maintain collegial support, limiting the sense of isolation. Use case consultation and supervision. Establish a "buddy" system. Join a study group, attend conferences. Undergo debriefing. Use outside professional services, i.e. counseling services provided by your job. Use peer counseling interventions.
10) Find a new "mission," and get involved at a local, state, or national level. Write about your stress; then, pick a coping skill and make a plan without excuses.

_____

_____

_____

_____

WHAT IT'S LIKE TO BE ME

Clients need to be able to communicate quickly with psychiatrists, psychologists, clinical social workers, counselors and PSR workers concerning issues which revolve around their psychiatric diagnoses. This is a chance for them to do a "Life Review" around the issues of a particular psychiatric disorder as it exists in an individual client.

Those of us who have never taken psychotropic medications do not really understand or know how it feels to function on several of these meds at a time. Keeping this straightened out is a primary function of the interaction between the therapist and the psychiatrist.

"What It's Like to Be Me" by _____.

First of all, I am a person who has _____.

I was first diagnosed in _____ by _____, but other people thought I might be _____ or _____.

My childhood with my family and/or caretakers was _____.

I was good at _____ when I was young, and enjoyed _____, _____, and _____. However, some difficult things happened to me, including _____

_____

and I knew I had a problem when _____

_____.

My life right now is like this. I live in a _____

_____.

I have this much to live on _____.

I spend it like this: _____

_____.

Here's my routine most days. _____

_____.

I'm on these medications: _____

_____.

My doctor and I _____.

Here's what it feels like to take the medications.
(Nausea? Dizziness? Diarrhea? In the sun? Sleeping? Eating? Energy?)
Have you ever gone off your medications as an adult? And what happened?

_____.

I have these goals for my life: Relationships? Marriage? Family? Job/Career? Travel? Education? Athletic? Home Ownership? _____

_____.

What would you like people to do most when they work with you? _____

POINT OF VIEW

On this page the concept of point of view is introduced into the analysis of a short story. In this exercise I want you to try to adopt another point of view by pretending to be somebody else and by writing in the first person point of view, using the pronoun "I" as you write. Write as someone with "opposite" life experiences than yourself, such as a liar, thief, a person of another race, a female, a male, someone you read about in the paper. If you're young, write as an old person; if you're old, write as a teenager.

Remember, point of view "tells us whose story it is. It refers to the eyes and mind through which actions are seen. You can also use second person (you) or third person points of view (he, she, it, one) to reflect different points of view, but using "I" puts you inside another person entirely.

A good way to start could be by reading the opening of Herman Melville's *Moby Dick*, and notice the way the first person gets you immediately into the story. "Call me Ishmael"…lets you know immediately whose story it is. Have your students try this:

"Call me Bob…I'm a twin (an alcoholic), a soldier" and begin a first person portrait of a man or woman in the hospital in a coma, at an AA meeting, or in Iraq.

_____

_____

_____

_____

POETRY READING, POETRY SLAM

I never really understood the pull, the attraction of poetry until I saw Robert Creely read live at San Francisco State University in the 60s. When you are young, you look for the energy of the life around you, and hopefully you follow it and find something there for yourself. The world of poetry can be found in street poetry, university poetry, rap, and modern song writing, a la Torrey Amos, and many other young writers who write their own music and lyrics.

From the eighth grade have any of your clients attend a poetry slam which features improvised street poetry. They can go to Boise State or any other university and attend poetry readings sponsored by the English Departments; they may show up at "open mike" poetry readings, or original song presentations. Writing or improvising for a slam can be a highly energizing activity for clients who have been to a slam and seen it in person. Poems can either be read from a manuscript, from memory, from a cocktail napkin, or made up on the spot.

TEACHING RAP AND HIP-HOP

I will never forget the moment I played the "Intro" from the Notorious BIG CD *Ready to Die* for the young Japanese students attending the Asia University America Program at Boise State University in 1998. "Intro" is about the life of a black man from birth, to domestic violence, to gangs, to crime, to prison, to release, and then to death (Arista Records, 1994) BIG and Tupak Shakur reportedly had a feud which was played out via their rap music, and they both have since been killed as a result of this conflict. Tupak allegedly had slept with BIG's wife, and the feud escalated out of control.

The words and samples were so powerful I was shocked. There was so much profanity I was lucky I wasn't in a public school and that the students did not know what the words meant. The students had already listened to rap and hip-hop. The content of rap (rap sheet, bad rap, etc.) was violence, sexism, profanity, materialism, struggles of the youth from the projects, crime, all played out on the musical stage.

A milder form of rap is done by Will Smith and earlier rappers. Almost every young client or student now can produce some rap to the right kind of drum sampler or drum machine. A brave instructor can bring an amp and drum machine to the music room and watch what happens. I have also used rhymed poetry from textbooks, put a beat to it, and then sung or rapped to it. That would at least merge some of the outside influences of your students and clients with the classroom environment.

The assignment: get out your *Norton Anthology of American Literature*, Volume 1, 1994. the works of Shakespeare, or any group of poems being taught, and find some that will fit with an instrumental CD with the right Hip-Hop rhythm. This will fill up the classroom or therapy session with energy and show them the relationship between rhythm, rhyme and meter without the dead silence which usually accompanies these concepts.

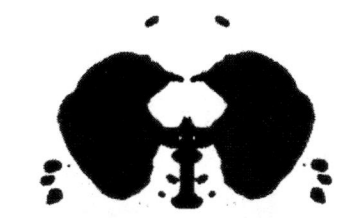

THE GARRITY METHOD FOR GROUP THERAPY OR FEEDBACK ON CREATIVE WRITING ASSIGNMENTS

Donald Garrity wrote a very good, slim, book about how group therapy feedback, creative writing and other composition courses should be run. The class, course or group is run in two phases. The first is the introduction of the project or assignment. The second is the workshop phase. On day one, the project is described verbally and in writing to the group members. Remember that statistic about people only remembering 25% of what they hear in a lecture? Then, students begin writing in class, and the instructor begins three to five minute coaching or feedback sessions with each individual student, reaching perhaps eight or nine students an hour. As the people work through their drafts, the instructor is familiar with particular problems they are having, he or she has given them the feedback they need, and marked a grade for their progress. In many instances, even a high school instructor with 120 students can give feedback to every student in a week (nine students times 20 hours).

Using this method prevents plagiarism and allows the therapist to review the writing before it's read aloud in group. In this model the leader plays the roles of cheerleader, coach and consultant, and finally referee and scorekeeper. The group members keep a portfolio, and no papers have to ever be taken home. Finished products can be read out loud to the whole group or to half the class, while the other half is still writing. Clients can share their writing by reading it out loud and gaining the effect of group therapy after having the group leader respond.

In this format, you start on the left side of the room as you face the chairs, and every day you pick up where you left off the previous day. Members know their turn is coming, and they have to have writing to show you. Students and clients are amazing! They can pace themselves that way, knowing when their turn is coming, and although they might slack during one session, they will be writing their tails off the next when it's their turn. This way there isn't a lot of talk about writing, the leader and group members are writing and getting feedback. Occasionally, if the leader sees a recurrent problem or misinterpretation of the assignment, it can be dealt with immediately. All grammar consulting can be done by playing the role of editor in specific situations. This uses everyone's time to the best advantage and takes the pressure off the leader to perform or do a dog and pony show. It's tremendously fulfilling to run a class or group this way and produces excellent writing. The leader changes hats from circus taskmaster to editor and consultant. Phrases counselors and teachers fear the most are, "I can't think of anything to write" and "I'm bored," or "this isn't working," or "If I knew how I felt, I wouldn't be here."

There is a passive-aggressive type who uses his ineptitude to frustrate the group leader; however, by asking questions, the behavior can be redirected. Here's how that can go. The headings are from Burns' *The Feeling Good Handbook*, p. 314.

Disarming—you find some truth in what the group member says. "It's a challenging assignment, so tell me what kind of conflict you have at home? Make notes while we talk."

Thought and feeling empathy—Paraphrase what the person is telling you. "I've seen you get blocked before, usually when an assignment is first introduced, but you always find a way once you get started."

Inquiry—Use gentle, probing questions to draw the member out. "Describe your major issues. Why is your spouse always criticizing you? Have you been verbally or physically abusive in the past? Remember the group and I don't know anything about your relationship. Can you make a list of questions people have about your marriage and how they see it?"

Use "I feel" statements—Let them know how you are feeling about their behavior, progress, attitude, or writing. "Sometimes I feel frustrated when you tell me you can't write in group, but if you wait until conference, I seem to have more patience."

Change the focus—Move from the content of the criticisms of the assignment, yourself, or relevance of the assignment, look at the process of interaction. "When you say 'Yes but…' I know now that's your way of asking for individual attention."

Stroking—Focus on the positive by either remembering past successes, or by selecting the best of his or her writing. "I really like this line here…we both watched our parents fight physically as children, and her we are doing the same. We need to break the cycle."

READING OUT LOUD

Once assignments are completed, have students or clients read them to you. In a creative writing class students are most amazed when one of their peers begins to unfold some writing that has been rewritten several times and it all comes together and is shared with the other students. It's one thing to haul out an E.B. White essay from a textbook, and another to see a talented peer "take off" in group.

This opens up the burdens of response from just leader to member, but sideways to everyone in the group. It brings in the performing element to the group which supplies energy and immediate feedback. You write your response in your record book and share it later with the student, or write it on your copy of the material or your progress notes. Running a course or group with the Garrity Method can create an atmosphere of trust and support where people can do their best work. When books talk about "voice" they rarely mean spoken voice. As students and clients read aloud, they find phrases they want to change, grammatical errors, misplaced examples; they also find strengths, humor, and grace of expression and use of vocabulary. Over and over again I have seen people find the "energy" of creative and other types of writing by using these group techniques.

THINKING ERRORS JOURNAL

This is a classic staple of Cognitive-Behavioral therapy. As you read through these thinking errors, pick out the ones which belong to you, and then keep a "Thinking Errors Journal" for a week, specifically making entries the moment you are aware of thinking, feeling or speaking one of these out loud.

1. Filtering: You take the negative details and magnify them while filtering out all positive aspects of a situation.

2. Polarized Thinking: Things are black or white, good or bad. You have to be perfect or you're a failure. There's no middle ground.

3. Overgeneralization: You come to a general conclusion based on a single incident or piece of evidence. If something bad happens once, you expect it to happen over and over again. "Joanne brushed me off today when I asked her to coffee. She hates me."

4. Mind Reading: This is a huge problem with overly romantic young women who are on the dating scene. Without their saying so, you know what people are feeling and why they act the way they do. You are able to divine how people are feeling towards you and you think they should divine the way you feel about them or certain issues.

5. Catastrophizing: You expect disaster. You notice or hear about a problem and start "what ifs." What if I lose my job? What if we lose the house?

6. Personalization: Thinking that everything people do or say is some kind of reaction to you. You also compare yourself to others, trying to determine who's smarter, better looking, and thinner, etc.

7. Control Fallacies: If you feel externally controlled, you see yourself as helpless, a victim of fate. The fallacy of internal control has you responsible for the pain and happiness of everyone around you.

8. Fallacy of Fairness: You feel resentful because you think you know what's fair, but other people won't agree with you.

9. Blaming: You hold other people responsible for your pain, or take the other tack and blame yourself for every problem or reversal.

10. Shoulds: You have a list of ironclad rules about how you and other people should act. People who break the rules anger you, and you feel guilty if you violate the rules.

11. Emotional Reasoning: You believe that what you feel must be true automatically. If you feel stupid and boring, then you must be stupid and boring.

12. Fallacy of Change: You expect that other people will change to suit you if you just pressure, manipulate, or cajole them enough. You need to change people because your hopes for happiness seem to depend entirely on them.

13. Global Labeling: You generalize one or two qualities into a negative global judgment.

14. Being Right: You are continually "on trial" to prove that your opinions and actions are correct. Bring wrong is unthinkable, and you will go to any lengths to demonstrate your rightness.

15 Heaven's Reward Fallacy: You expect all your sacrifice and self-denial to pay off, as if there were someone keeping score (God? Sorry, I couldn't help it.)

I would like to finish this book with some snippets from Patrick Carnes' workshop "Stepping Out of the Shadows of Cybersex and Sexual Addictions" which he presented in Boise, Idaho, March 31, 2004. It was an inspiring workshop, dealing with a topic which I have begun to see take hold during the past ten years or so, a disorder which falls roughly into the category of Sex Addiction Treatment. It also demonstrates the dark side of the Internet of all of us. Carnes reported that he had recently had bypass surgery and that he was going to retire and take it easy for a while. The information in the packet was called "Coming to Your Own Assistance" and it has been helpful to me in motivating me to start and complete this project. Each of the paragraphs to follow was significant to me spiritually although they were meant for drug, alcohol, and Internet/sex addicts to guide them in their recovery. I have abstracted them from Carnes' workshop materials. Thank you for reading my book. The greatest sin in my world is wasting someone's time, and I hope this was worth yours. Carnes encouraged everyone in the seminar to begin writing his or her own book or curriculum in order to expand the parameters of one's work with clients. I have been putting this project together hoping to work with young counselors and therapists in the future.

COMING TO YOUR OWN ASSISTANCE

Write your response to the statements as "prompts," as if someone who cared about you were asking you these questions. This series works for addicts in recovery, or can be used as mantras with those in helping professions who have lost touch with their own "flow."

Addictions are phantom optimums. They perform the same function.

In essence it is drinking God from a bottle. _____

Identify and amplify "flow" in your life. Live in the anxiety. Train for it. _____
_____

Make a decision to come to your own assistance. _____

There will always be stress. Beware of the shadow side—the mirror effect. _____
_____

Surround yourself with people who believe in you more than you do yourself. _____
_____

Accept that you deserve more than you need—without that you have no reserves. _____
_____

Notice what you are actually doing—a clue to our intention or our avoidance. (This one helped me slough away hours watching television. When I think this thought, I get up and write or play music.)
_____

Why there is no change: we see clearly there's a problem, we know what to do, we won't do it. _____
_____

You have to decide. _____

Culture of deferred living: pay later, retire later, relationships later, the denial of death.
_____

What should you start? What should you finish? _____

The most critical decisions are made without knowing the outcome will be. _____
_____

"I take the ring though I do not know the way" (Frodo Baggins). _____
_____

Be prepared to go places you've never imagined. _____

AFTERWORD

Although I have tried to focus this book on "rubber-meets-the road" exercises which, for the most part, are at the level of clients in therapy and mostly beginning level writers, I did discover an intellectual cohort in Wendy Bishop, Ph.D., who was a professor in the Writing Program Administration Program at Florida State University in Tallahassee, Florida. Any counselor who has doubts about using writing in therapy should read her article "Writing Is/And Therapy?: Raising Questions about Writing Classrooms and Writing Program Administration" in *the journal of advanced composition*. Dr. Bishop approaches the problem from the writing teacher's point of view, wondering if that teacher should investigate the therapeutic and affective aspects of teaching writing.

Bishop's essay describes the interaction between teacher and student, the therapeutic aspect of early experiences on authors, and the proposition that the self is the subject of most writing to some degree. Unfortunately, Dr. Bishop passed away several years ago, and I know of few others in academia who share my point of view, especially from the English teacher's side of things.

A second important movement from the counselor's point of view is the emergence of Narrative Therapy, developed during the 70s and 80s by Australian Michael White and David Epston of New Zealand. It holds that our identities are shaped by the accounts of our lives found in our stories or narratives. In this framework, writing journals, autobiographies, poetry, fiction help others fully describe their rich stories and trajectories. For further investigation, read *Narrative Means to Therapeutic Ends* published in the 90s.

NOTES

EXAMPLES OF A CLIENT-WRITTEN NEWSLETTER AND THERAPIST-LED WRITING GROUP

Creative Writing for Counselors and Their Clients - Steve Flick M.F.A., LCSW

The Wild Bunch News

PUBLISHER: The Rocky Mountain Wild Bunch

Volume: #1   Issue: #3   August 15th - August 31st   2004

My Best Friend
Submitted By Sandra H.

My best friend, that I have known for about 3 years is, Sonia. We are very close friends, she is like a sister to me. She brings joy into my life. We spoil each other to death. She is the sweetest person I've ever known. She is honest, generous and kind. Sonia has been there for me through thick and thin. When I have problems going on in my life she is there for me. We go shopping and out to lunch together. She makes me laugh and cry over happy things and sad times I have with my family. If I'm stressed out she is there for me and talks to me about the problems that are stressing me out. She is the best friend I have ever had.

Thank You Sonia, I Love You!!!

My Fishing Trip
Submitted By Bobby C.

I went out fishing on a boat and looked in the water and saw a big stone. I put down my fishing pole and jumped in the water to get a better look at the stone and saw another stone in it. It was so beautiful. I picked it up and swam back to the boat and put the stone in the boat. I found out later that it wasn't a stone in it but an old kernel of corn in the stone. I then went back to fishing and caught myself a big fish and had a great time after all.

NO ONE NEEDS A VACATION AS MUCH AS THE PERSON WHO JUST HAD ONE.
                ANN LANDERS

Why Do People Hurt Other People?
Submitted By Michelle T.

Why do people hurt other people? I believe that people do it because they feel that they are more power- ful. People feed off each others behavior. I have never understood other peoples' behavior, and it's not my job to. I, myself, have lost a lot of friends by hurting them. I was so selfish I did not care who I hurt. I have really learned new behavior. I have also been hurt by a lot of people and I have held grudges. I have done this thing that I call Push and Pull. When people get too close to me I push them away, then I pull them back into my life. I guess I manipulate to get them back into my life. I know that I am not the only one who does this kind of behavior but I have also learned a lot through counseling, case managers and PSR workers. So it pays to listen to people who care about you. I have also learned to respect myself and others. I have learned many things from my friends in group. The staff here at Rocky Mountain Resources are just awesome. Rocky Mountain is the best "Day Treatment Program" that I have ever been to. I have learned a lot from this group and its members. If it wasn't for Rocky Mountain Resources I would just be sitting at home and isolating myself. Thank You Staff, And Neat Group.

**THE ROCKY MOUNTAIN
" WILD BUNCH "**

Listening
Submitted By Jay J.

Listening is a skill. Communication requires the ability to listen. The better you listen the better you will communicate. Truth is not required to communicate but listening is. As we develop listening skills we listen to lies and all kinds of information that disagrees with us. If you develop listening skills well enough you will be able to tell the difference between lies and the truth by the tickle in your hair, although to be a good communicator you can't always react to what you hear another say. You might only have to just listen.

DRUGS ARE DEADLY

JOIN THE FIGHT!

To My Best Friend
(You Were Always There)
Submitted By Barbara S.
They say that dog is man's best friend
But that simply cannot be
Because you were so much more
Than just a friend to me

When I was growing up
And no one seemed to care
And I needed someone
You were always there

When I needed a shoulder
to rest my head from wear
And I needed someone to listen
You were always there

When I hurt myself in school
Or the teasing kids I could not bear
And I needed someone to cry on
You were always there

When I was sad or lonely hearted
And I was in despair
Or when I was feeling overcome
You were always there

When others turned their backs
And I didn't want to hear
And I needed someone to talk to
You were always there

When I was scared at night
Of all the monsters there
And needed some protection
You were always there

When I found my first love
And felt the need to share
Everything I was feeling
You were always there

When I needed advice
Someone to make it clear
Someone to walk me through
You were always there

When I felt my first heart break
And my soul began to tear
And I needed some support
You were always there

When I finally graduated
And was happy beyond compare
I wanted someone to celebrate with
You were always there

When the road got rough
And I knew not here nor there
I needed someone to guide me
You were always there

And so dear friend we've seen it all
We made it from there to here
We grew up together
We look on together without fear

For as long as you are with me
In my heart and soul
I feel there's nothing I can't do
There's nowhere I can't go

So thank you for everything you've done
Because of you I grew up sensible and fair
And thank you most of all
For always being there
I'll love you always and forever.
(Submitted By Diane Jackson who said "My son wrote this poem on the day his best friend, his Black Lab, "DIXIE" died.

Father's Day
Submitted By Sandra H.
 Father's Day is a special day to be with your dad. Dads are a breed apart. They are always there for you. When you need to talk about stuff dads are there for you. If you go fishing a dad will take you fishing. If you need a leading hand your dad is always there for you. That is why it's special to have a very special person to call Dad.

SOME KIDS TODAY HAVE A STRANGE VIEW OF HISTORY- THEY THINK " B.C. " MEANS "BEFORE CABLE".

Road Trip
Submitted By James B.
 I wish that I could go on a road trip "to who knows where" with friends that I care about and have a lot of fun with them. My friends, Sandra, Joe, and Michelle are good people. I feel that they are helping me a lot in my stress management and basically everything else all around.

"THE MOST IMPORTANT THING TO SUCCEED IN SHOW BUSINESS IS SINCERITY. AND IF YOU CAN FAKE THAT, YOU'VE GOT IT MADE."

The Fear And The Pain
Submitted By Dennis C.
Although I bear the fear and the pain,
I shed the tears like rain,
For the woman I once loved and thought I had.
I still miss her very much and the pain of remembering her makes me very sad.
She was so loving and mystical,
Her eyes showed the spirit of an angel.
She caused within me
 a spark of life,
I wanted to make her my wife.
Wow! What a spark,
I wage a war within me against the spirits of the dark.
In time I know it will heal,
But still it does not change the way I really feel.
I want her back so very much.
But like they say " THAT IS LIFE AND IT IS AS SUCH."
Moral: "Do not let a feeling break your heart."

A Trip To Remember
Submitted By Debbie S.

When I was about ten, I was living up towards Yellow Pine in a tent because my Dad was cutting logs. It was the Fourth of July and a lot of family got together to celebrate. A few of us decided to go fishing. There was a hidden lake. Dad was catching 8 and 10 inches and I took and went on the other side to fish on a big rock. I cast my line way out and a big fish followed it back to shore then took off. I cast it back out and it landed a foot in front of him and I got him on. I was so excited, I was hollering to Dad I got a big one, I got a big one. He was hollering back turn your pole over. I could not hear what he was saying though. I had a glass eyed fishing pole with a crack in it. I reeled in the 24 plus pounder about 2 ft. from the bank and as you probably guessed by now my line cut. I ran and grabbed the fish and threw it up on the bank. My dad made me pack it out up a big hill. That night he fileted my fish. I sat on the bank and started to cry because I wanted to enter it in a contest. I really had fun that day and I know that I will remember it and re-tell it many times, over and over, every chance that I get.

The Best Of Times
Submitted By Clark S.

The best times in my life were when I graduated from high school and went to Disneyland and I rode all the rides. Another time was when I went Deep Sea Fishing with my father and I caught my limit of Salmon, I can't quite remember what kind but I do know that I had one heck of a swell time.

My Cats
Submitted By Sue C.

Samantha Lynn and Bobbie Lynn Mattox have special personalities which are: Bobbie is the oldest and she likes to sleep under the covers with me and chases the other cats away and watches over Samantha. Samantha likes to sleep by my head and on my chest. I miss them so much because I have gotten so attached to them. When I think of them I usually start crying because I miss them dearly.   I'm their MOM.

How I Lost The Man I Love
Submitted By Michelle T.

Joe and I have been dating for about 2 months and he is my whole world. But we have had to end our relationship. I did not think I would ever love someone as friends much as I love Joe. I am hurting so bad. I miss Joe, having him hugging me and his sweet and tender loving kisses. Most of all the way he loved me, His treatment of me as a woman. Joe is a very good man. We had to end our relationship because someone told the both of us that we could not date. We will of course remain close friends and we are willing to wait. This has affected the both of us in so many different ways that we never saw them coming. I will wait FOREVER if need be. We know in our hearts that God was the one that brought us together with his Love. know that in his all knowing Love and reasons that we were born to be together for each others Love to share our lives as man and wife, as he so created Adam and Eve. I will Love Joe for always and in all ways.

Summer
Submitted By Sandra H.

Summer is a beautiful season. There are flowers growing in all the people's yards, all kinds of multi-colored trees blooming. The birds are tsinging their favorite songs, the animals running about, teasing each other and having fun. The children playing in their little plastic pools. Sprinklers are running with their all to familiar clickitty - clickitty - clicks. That is why I think that summer is a very   Special Fun Time, Of The Year.

Seasons Of Life
Submitted By Laverna W.

To every thing there is a season, and a time to every purpose under heaven

A time to be born, and a time to die a time to plant, and a time to pluck up that which is planted.

A time to kill and a time to heal, a time to break down, and a time to build up,

A time to cast away stones and a time to gather stones together, a time to embrace, and a time to refrain from embracing,

A time to get, and a time to lose, a time to keep, and a time to cast away,

A time to rend, and a time to sew, a time to keep silence, and a time to speak,

A time to love, and a time to hate, a time to war, and a time of peace.

Ecclesiastes 3 - 1 -8

Farewell
Submitted By Judy S.
         M.S.W. STUDENT
To the Clients and Staff at Rocky Mountain Resources:

I want to thank you for allowing me to attend and share your Saturday group these past ten weeks. I wish you all the best in your future. KEEP UP THE HARD WORK!!

         Sincerely, Judy S.

Hello Group
Submitted By Michael D.

I have spent the last 5 years with Valerie. She is my Universe, my hopes, and my strengths. I will love her Forever and ever. God blessed me so much with her and my stepchildren, Travis, who is 13 and Justin, 17. They get great grades in school, A's and B's. I am so proud of my family. My life is better than I ever could have dreamed it could be. Thank You Darling Valerie for making me "THE HAPPIEST MAN ALIVE"

I was a stunt man when I was 17. A Carpenter for 3 years, an Electrician for 3 years and a Maintenance Tech. For a hotel. I just moved here from Boise and I hope that we can be friends. My hobbies are 2-way radios, music. I want to join the Peace Corps. So that I can go back to Panama to continue my Missionary work.

Happiness is not a Goal: It is a Bi-Product. *Eleanor Roosevelt*

Walking My Dog (Mica)
Submitted By David S.

Well the day started out pretty good. I got up early to get ready, with my best pal Mica by my side. "It's the big day" I told her. We had made plans for a giant walk to the Caldwell High School. We ate a big breakfast and off we were on our long walk. We walked and walked, Mica just loves to go walking. I got tired but not her. We try to walk every day, I just love to see her so happy walking. It is our "Quality Time" together.

"If you want truly to understand something, try to change it."

My Doctors Visit
Submitted By Dennis C.

Well here goes, I went to the Dr. and they took 5 vials of blood from my left arm. They did an E.K.G. and my heart is doing O.K. They told me that the chances of my having diabetes is really high and that has me worried a lot. But that is something that I will have to learn to live with, for the rest of my life, if it is true. Basically it will involve many major life-style changes, and let me tell you that I do not care for changes not one little bit. I am scared but I know that with the right Meds and therapy that everything will work out fine for me in the long haul.

My True, Forever Friend
Submitted By Dayna M.

My True, Forever Friend

I found a true, forever friend
the day that I found You,
And Lord, I can't give thanks enough
for all the things You do.
You shower me with blessings,
not a day am I without ....
The things I am in need of;
There's no reason I should doubt.
When days are dark and dreary,
and my spirits are brought low,
You give words of peace and comfort
to my body, mind, and soul.
When I stumble by the wayside;
when I've surely lost my way,
Lovingly, You take my hand,
that I shall not be led astray.
Through trials and tribulations,
when my faith is growing weak,

You renew my hope and courage,
for it's Your strength that I seek.
When dangers lurk about me,
as the enemy draws near,
Safety in Your arms awaits me,
there dispelling dread and fear.
Blessed am I, tho' so unworthy,
to have found a friend so true.
Greater love could no man offer;
no one cares for me like You.

Diana Sue Helmer

Chronic Fatigue
Submitted By Leonard H.

Chronic Fatigue, Depression, too, is a possibility. "Workaholics" invariably commit an enormous investment of energy to their work. Over time, this may lead to a life-style imbalance, such people begin to realize – often on a subconscious level – that life is passing them by. They may regret failing to devote more time to home and family, hobbies and vacations. This can be a depressing realization.

As they approach retirement, as I am, such Workaholics may become aware of "UNFINISHED BUSINESS", they can even become apprehensive about the future, which may appear to be bleak, because they have devoted so much effort to their jobs and so little attention to other endeavors. Depression can result. Bad things happen to good people all the time. Putting this together with my other works on depression, and in group activities, brings me closer in touch with me, myself and group. My own illness being "PUT ON THE BACK BURNER" as I like to say it, and it gets overlooked in my enthusiasm trying to help others with their problems, or pointing them in the right direction to get the right help that they need. I must always remember that I am not a doctor, and my limited experiences does not qualify me as such. I just want to thank the Staff here at Rocky Mountain Resources and that great group THE WILD BUNCH, for all their help in teaching me the vast variety of emotions and how to handle situations as they arise. I would like more articles from you concerning your illness, questions concerning Meads, or any story or joke, EXCEPT XXX.

Nampa Bowl

[Bowling scoresheets for Gilbert, Leonardo, Brice across three games, and Joe, Michelle, James across three games on 7/22/04]

My Bowling Experience
Submitted By Michelle

We went bowling. I have not been so lucky while bowling, I have always gotten gutter balls but on that day I can actually say I was bowling. Amanda brought it to my attention that I was turning my hand the wrong way when I released the ball. She taught me how to hold the ball and the right way to throw it. I bowled with Joe and James, I won the game and also broke 100, I got 102. In the third game I got 99. James won the first and third games. I owe all that I know about bowling to Amanda. Oh! also we had the baby bumpers, Joe and James felt sort of stupid but when it was over we all had a great time.

Hey! How About Those scores?
Submitted by Leonard H.

Boy Howdy !!!. Did we ever have a real terrific time, as usual. Our appreciation for this chance to go out "ON THE TOWN," so to speak, Mike A. If you are reading this let us take this time out to congratulate You on your endeavors in forming this awesome Adventure that you and your hand picked excellent staff have created for us. I for one know what it takes to put something like this together. I know that I wasn't wrong in putting my life, the rest of it, into your very capable and caring hands. I wish only the very best of continued success in all that you chose for yourself and yours. It is so great to be an active participant right from day one. I am so proud to be able to call EVERY ONE of you FRIEND.

Advice from the late night crowd
Submitted by Readers Digest

My favorite story tellers, Bill Cosby and Jay Leno, always draw a vivid picture while they work. Good details, language command, good acting. They use voices ...and they have their own voice. The bad story - teller says to an audience after bombing, "You had to be there." The good story teller makes you think you were there.   Arsenio Hall

The most important thing is to keep it short. It's like knowing when to leave the in Vegas. Get your laugh or, if you're lucky, laughs, and then get off the stage. If you don't trust yourself, hire a friend to tackle you after four minutes.   CONAN O'BIEN

That does it for this issue. REMEMBER!! NOW is the time to start on handing in those articles, poems, stories, questions about meds

THE ROCKY MOUNTAIN
" WILD BUNCH "

Overwhelmed
Submitted by Thomas ?.

The first time I felt overwhelmed was the time I was playing football. I was playing quarterback and I flicked the ball to the running back on a halfback toss and ran to the corner right, defended by corner backs and the running back threw it long and I dove into a puddle of mud but I caught it for the winning touchdown. The second time I felt overwhelmed was when a friend, a drug lord, loaned me his car and I found myself in hot pursuit from the police because they recognized the car. I escaped and later discovered that there was at the time a 9mm handgun hidden under the front seat. The third time was when my girlfriend proposed to me but I left and went to California where I thought I could make quick money being a salesman.

"The sign of a good manager is the ability to give and take negative feedback" **Richard Pascal**

I called my son one day, a sophomore at Mars Hill Collage in North Carolina, and heard this message on his answering machine *A is for academics, B is for beer It's one of these reasons we are not here.* Startled by his poem, I left him my own in response: *M is for mom, G is for groan If you don't change your message, you're soon coming home!*

RELATIONSHIPS
Can You Find These Words?

QUALITIES
PARTNER
CARETAKERS
UNDERSTANDING
IMPULSIVE
PLEASING
CONFLICTING
RELATIONSHIP
DEFEND
WITHDRAW
ATTACK
COMMUNICATION
NAGGING
BEGGING
IGNORING
DISAGREEING

OPPOSITE
ATTEMPTS
SOLVE
SELFISHNESS
DISTANCING
JEALOUSY
CONTROL
SEPARATIONS
HUGS
MESSAGES
FLOWERS
CARDS
DISTURBS
BELIEFS
PROBLEMS

Creative Writing for Counselors and Their Clients - Steve Flick M.F.A., LCSW

Writing News

SPECIAL EDITION FOR HELPING PROFESSIONALS **SPRING EDITION, MARCH 2003**

Dear Friends and Colleagues:

You can join us. Sometimes the Early Writers focus on creative expression. Other times we play with the absurd. Often times, we simply try to find any word that will convey our thoughts or feelings.

Wartime. A group of solemn helping professionals wrote together on the first morning of the Iraqi war. Pens scratched words of fear and disillusionment, frustration and uncertainty. Finding words to express powerful emotions challenged each of us.

Springtime. Outside the conference room, an apple tree flaunted a bouquet of pink blossoms. We faced an implausible contradiction. Spring flowers, and the company of compassionate others, offered equilibrium. We put pen to paper again to pay tribute to hope even in the face of the conflict.

Wartime, springtime, troubled times, peace times – every season offers fertile soil for thought and a rich territory for journal writing. Perhaps you, too, want a safe harbor for support. Maybe you hope to learn more about yourself, or simply to play with creativity. There are no prerequisites – no writing expertise, no grammar test or spelling exam. If you work as a therapist, a social worker, or a pastor, this is an invitation to join us on the Write Path for Professionals. We meet from 7AM-9AM – an ideal time to focus on personal writing. Our next session runs from Thursday, April 10 – May 19. Please call me for more information at 385-0888. Best wishes to all. Sue

What's Inside?

Registration for Spring Writing Groups

Order Form for Write Path Journals and Gift Certificates

Write Try – A Creative Writing Exercise for You to Enjoy

Look Who's Writing? – Trava Mayes Offers A Playful Piece from a WP Group

Boise is Generous

FAQ about Writing Groups

Who Said That?

Inspiration came looking for me, but I was listening to the weather report. I was counting out my vitamins. I was leafing through the Daytimer-catalog, wondering if I should order a new appointment book. Inspiration got tired of waiting.
– Sy Safransky, editor of "The Sun."

Gifts

Do you need a gift for a birthday, Mother's Day, Father's Day, Passover, Easter, or any other occasion? Here are two gift suggestions from the Write Path.

Gift Certificates Available

Purchase a gift certificate to give to a friend for a Write Path class or retreat. Certificates are available for the amount of your choice. Contact Rachel at 385-0888 or complete the order form inside.

Journals

Encourage creative expression with a Write Path Journal. The new journals include 100 blank pages on high quality paper and how-to articles for journalers. Add a nice pen and you have a great gift. Each journal costs $8.00 or buy two for $15.00. Stop by our office or return the order form on page 3. All proceeds go to the Write Path Scholarship Fund.

~ FOR CLIENT REFERRALS ~

Transformation: Spring to Life on the Write Path

Groups Begin on April 8th & 9th
If you can make a list, you can keep a journal.

From a chrysalis of hidden thought Spring Monarch wings of poetry.

Springtime – a time for new life and transformation – a season of bunnies and butterflies – a time to plant unremarkable seeds which blossom into extraordinary flowers. So it is in nature. So it is in our lives.

The Write Path follows two garden trails; one is a path of personal growth or metamorphosis and the other a course of creativity. These footpaths run parallel, then meet and join as one. Your written thoughts plant seeds of confidence. As self-assurance takes root, words flower on the page and your imagination blossoms. Growth and creativity meld into a one transforming pathway.

You deserve to plant seeds for creative growth, emotional transformation, or a spiritual awakening.

Join others who are pursuing the same goal on the Write Path. Think springtime. Think transformation.

All groups are facilitated by Susan Reuling Furness, LCPC, LMFT, Writing Therapist. Register inside. Save $$$ before April 1st.

Writing News is published now and then by Susan Reuling Furness, LCPC
Jefferson Street Counseling and Consulting • 1517 W. Jefferson Street • Boise, Idaho 83702 • 208-385-0888 • jeffersoncounsel@aol.com

Write Try

Personal Writing is Never Monotonous.
Never, if you let your artist play in your journal.

I would like to know if others go through the same things that I do,
have as many selves as I have, and see themselves similarly.
– from "We Are Many," Pablo Neruda.

For your safety and convenience, I drew a map to myself, with several alternate routes, all marked.
The map comes complete with warning signs in red: Severe Avalanche Danger, Careful Not to
Awaken Sleeping Obsessions, Dungeons of Troubling Memories, Vast Pit of Need.
I did not forget to mark the attractions, the sights not to be missed: Bizarro House of
Illusions, Library of Revisionist Personal History, Portrait Gallery of Lost Love.
– from "Map to Myself," N.A. Henry

Here is an idea for unusual self-exploration. Fantasize for a moment – you create a map to help others decipher your personality. Begin by making a list of sub-personalities. (Hint: my map has many opposites such as "the dreamer" and "the pragmatist," "the optimist" and "the pessimist." Perhaps you'll decide to give your sub-parts names like N.A. Henry (above.) Now, picture a road atlas, a wilderness guide, a globe, a travelogue, or an aerial map of the San Diego Zoo. Might one of these set a poem or short essay in motion? Start writing as fast as you can. Don't pause to edit. You may come back to this many times, but remember to limit your writing to twenty or thirty minutes at one sitting.

Look Who's Writing

www.adventureget-way
by Trava Mayes

Thank you for contacting my website for information about the Adventure Get-Away. You want to know where to go and how to get there to see Me. What a trip you'll have! You also noted in your request that you were looking for accommodations and services.

First on the map, take Lost Child Lane to the end of Traumaville to tour the Early Years. One of the incredible sites along the way would be Poverty Pit where Loss and Alcoholism meet. Though you might not wish to stay in the pit, a look over its edge could give you the adventurer's rush you are seeking.

Wholesome accommodations do exist nearby in Nature's Nurture with its bubbling streams, abundant wildlife, colorful birds, rich smell of Appalachian earth, green lush vines, a freedom of blue-gray skies and bee-humming air all promising to revive and refresh you.

Once past Lost Child Lane, turn right to Teenage Angstville to see a full array of disappointments and fears. Though pretty cheap accommodations exist at Liar's Lair—it's not the Ritz—many things just aren't what they seem. The proprietors tell you one thing and give you another which can send you right down Baffle Boulevard. If you choose Baffle Boulevard, expect to deal with lots of potholes and broken pavement.

You might wish to detour Baffle Boulevard and take a left on Hope Highway. You can take the same escape route I used to get out of Teen Angstville.

Once past Teen Angstville, you can find the big sign to Broken Heart Ranch. This dude facility offers you lots of thrills and spills. Dress for a rough and tough time. Accommodations are rustic and sparse, so if you like the gentle life, you may not want to visit this ranch.

Weeping Woman Bluff is just ahead. It's quite an overlook into dizzying depths. Lots of waterfalls and mists arise from below, and some visitors have reported that the place is haunted.

Or come with me now to rest your tired, aching bones at Mature Woman's Manor. Though the accommodations seem modest, thrills not common, there's a quietude and peacefulness for the weary traveler.

The Write Path

Private Writing Retreats and Programs

Would you like to arrange a writing retreat for friends, your staff, or another organization? Sue Reuling Furness facilitates retreats using writing to discover focus and purpose for individuals and/or teams. Sue will tailor the event to meet the needs of your group.

In-town or out-of-town gatherings can be arranged. Most retreats last 8 – 12 hours, but shorter programs also work. As you plan your calendar, consider a writing retreat. More information, call 385-0888.

Troubled Times

If we could read the secret history of our enemies we should find in each person's life sorrow and suffering enough to disarm all hostility.
- Henry Wadsworth Longfellow

There's a place in my brain/ where hate won't grow./ I touch its riddle: wind, and seeds./ Something pokes us as we sleep.
- Naomi Shihab Nye

Boise is Generous

As a reflection of your generosity, several writers received partial scholarships in the 2003 winter session. Since its inception in 2001, the scholarship fund has **helped** sponsor more than 20 people on the Write Path.

If you are able to share your abundance, please make *a tax-deductible* contribution. A Write Path Journal comes your way for a gift of $50. Gift-givers who contribute at the $200 level receive Gabrielle Rico's book, <u>Writing the Natural Way</u> (or an acceptable alternative) and a Write Path journal. Make your check payable to Susan Reuling Furness – WP Fund. If you wish to learn more about receiving a scholarship, please call us at 385-0888.

Registration and Order Form

Name _____   Phone Number (h) _____
Address _____   Phone Number (o) _____
City_____; ID Zip_____   Phone Number (c) _____

For Your Referrals:
SPRING TO LIFE ON THE WRITE PATH
~ *8-Week Group, Starting April 8/9* ~ *3 Available Class Times* ~

CLASS TIMES:
- ☐ Tuesdays, April 8 – May 27, 2003; 9:00 AM – 11:00 AM (or)
- ☐ Tuesdays, April 8 – May 27, 2003; 5:00 PM – 7:00 PM (or)
- ☐ Wednesdays, April 9 – May 28, 2003; 5:00 PM – 7:00 PM

REGISTRATION:
- ☐ PRE-REGISTRATION: $175, when paid in full before March 21
- ☐ EARLY BIRD: $200, when paid in full before April 1
- ☐ SLEEPY BIRD: $225, after April 1

WRITE PATH JOURNALS

Please Send _____ **Journals** ($8.00 each; 2 for $15.00) _____
Shipping & Handling ($2.00 for each journal ordered) _____
Please Send a Gift Certificate for $ _____
Subtotal _____
I wish to give a **Tax-deductible Gift** *to The WP Scholarship Fund* _____
TOTAL _____

PAYMENT:
- ☐ Enclosed is my check for _____
- ☐ Visa/MC _____ expires _____

Signature _____

~ *Thank You* ~

F.A.Q. about Writing Groups

Who attends the Write Path Writing Groups? Adult men and women who want to understand life's challenges and wish to discover creative approaches to life itself.

What is a journal-writing group? 6-10 members bring journals, pens, and enthusiasm together each week.

Why join a writing group? Surround yourself with people striving toward the same goals. Gain from the encouragement, fellowship, and mutual support. Uncover constructive answers for your past, present and future dilemmas.

What happens when I get there? Yep, everyone writes in his or her journal.

But there is much more. The leader tickles your imagination with a theme, perhaps a probing question, and samples of other's writing. The timer is set and everyone writes lickety-split thoughts in their journal. The best part happens when volunteers share their spontaneous writing with the group. The group is committed to giving support to the reader. Criticism is not allowed. There is no pressure to share your writing although sharing always feels good.

What if I can't write? Everyone can but many of us got discouraged in school. Education and past experience do not matter. We spend early meetings silencing the voice of the internal editor (who is often an old English teacher chastising us to never dangle a participle, except we can't recognize a participle even when it isn't dangling). Journal writing is about the free expression of your thoughts and feelings; not about performance, grammar, or sentence construction. In the same breath, group members often discover they are good writers.

Who benefits? Anyone interested in helping themselves and others. Anyone interested in positive feelings and improved confidence. Anyone interested in stimulating his or her creative juice. Anyone who wants to use a journal for greater peace of mind.

How will it help? There is magic in the process. Over time group members discover greater confidence and quicker resolutions to their trials and tribulations. There is neuroscience in journal writing too. Writing releases negative brain energy stored from hurtful experiences and allows more positive attitudes to emerge.

Will I have fun? Will I want to come back? Yes! Yes! And you'll want to bring your friends too.

INFLUENTIAL WORKS

    Aristotle: The Poetics, Modern Library Press
    Banta, Larry: "Voice Management Guidelines," client handout 2006
    Berne, Eric: What do you Say after you say Hello
    Bishop, Wendy: Writing Is/And Therapy? (Journal of Advanced Composition, 13.2)
    Blake, William: Songs of Innocence
    Bly, Robert: Iron John
    Burns, David: The Feel Good Handbook
    Cameron, Julia: The Artist's Way
    Camus: The Fall
    Carnes, Patrick: Stepping out of the Shadows of Cybersex and Sexual Additions and workshop handouts
    Cheever, John: The Collected Short Stories
    Csikszentmihalyi, Mihaly: Creativity: Flow and the psychology of Discovery and Invention
    Death, The Business of: A & E Television, "Investigative Reports," 1999
    Deluca, Phil: Couple's Therapy with an Uncooperative Partner
    Dunn, Rita: How People Learn, St. John's University Press
    Elbow, Peter: Writing with Power
    Erikson, Erik H.: Identity, Youth and Crisis, 1968
    Fitzgerald: The Great Gatsby
    Flick, Stephen: Teller's Last Band, The Feeling Process: A workbook for Men
    Friedman: Psychodynamic Family Systems, 1980
    Freud, Sigmund: The Interpretation of Dreams and The Psychopathology of Everyday Life
    Ginsberg, Alan: Howl
    Glouberman, Dina: The Joy of Burnout
    Haller, Sonia: "For journalers, writing salves pain," Arizona Republic, 2006
    Hankins, Gary and Carol: Prescription for Anger, 1993
    Harris, Thomas: I'm OK, You're OK
    Health Canada: "Schizophrenia: A Handbook for Families, 1997
    Hemingway, Ernest: "The Short Happy Life of Francis McComber"
    Hesse, Herman: Steppenwolf, Siddartha
    Humphries, Derek: Final Exit
    Irving, John: The World According to Garp
    Janov, Arthur: The Primal Scream, 1970
    Jung, Carl: Man and His Symbols
    Kesey, Ken: One Flew over the Cuckoo's Nest
    Kubler-Ross, Elizabeth: On Death and Dying
    Landreth, Gary: Children's Play Therapy
    McKay, Davis, Fanning: Thoughts and Feelings: Taking control of your Moods and your Life
    McLuhan, Marshall: Understanding Media
    Meares, Washington, Welch: School Social Work, 1996
    Michenbaum, Donald: A Clinical Handbook/Practical Therapist Manual for PTSD, 1994
    National Institute of Mental Health Pamphlets: Major Mental Disorders
    Nemeth, Maria: The Energy of Money
    Nin, Anais: Diaries
    Norton Anthology of American Literature
    Pennebaker, James: Two Decades of Studies on Journals, University of Texas Press
    Pirsig, Robert: Zen and the Art of Motorcycle Maintenance
    Progoff, Ira The Progoff Journal
    Rabun, Joanne-Todd: www.scrapbooking.com. 1993 and Idaho Senior News.

Schiraldi: The PTSD Sourcebook, 2000
Sheehey, Gail: The New Passages
Springer and Deutsch: Left-Brain, Right Brain
Stone, Arthur: "Day Reconstruction Method," Science, 12/3/04
Surgeon General's Report on Mental Health, 2000
Van Gogh, Vincent: Letters to Theo
Viscott, David: The Viscott Method, 1984
Vonnegut, Kurt: Cat's Cradle
White, Michael: Narrative Means to Therapeutic Ends
Whitman, Walt: Leaves of Grass
Wood, Samuel and Ellen: The World of Psychology, 1996
Writer's Digest: www.writersdigest.com/writingprompts.asp 2002
Yim, Su-Jin: "How to Seek Help," Oregonian, 10/28/01

ABOUT THE AUTHOR

Steve Flick, M.F.A., LCSW,
was born in Kansas but raised in California. He attended San Francisco State University, San Jose S.U., Stanford, University of Montana, Humboldt State University and Boise State University, where he received his Master's in Social work and then became a licensed clinical social worker. He has worked with sexually abused children, clients with psychiatric disorders, couples, families in crisis, adolescents, and the aged. He has written several books along the way: The Feeling Process: A Workbook for Men, Teller's Last Band, (a novel); Speed Writing: A Workbook for College Composition; The C.O. (a novel); and now Creative Writing for Counselors and their Clients. He has won fellowships from the federal government, IV-E Grand for at risk kids, and the Wallace Stegner Creative Writing Fellowship at Stanford University. He has been a counselor for fifteen years in Boise, Idaho, most recently with All Seasons Mental Health, and lives there with his wife Loretta who is a silversmith.

Special Thanks:

Dogstar Creative and McCabe Christian for the design of this book.

Dogstar Creative, LLC.
www.dogstarcreative.com
info@dogstarcreative.com

Loretta Pompeii Flick, Silversmith, Wife, Partner. This couldn't have been done without you.